*Bass Fishing
on Shore and Sea*

BASS FISHING
on Shore and Sea

John Darling

The Crowood Press

First published in 1996 by
The Crowood Press Ltd
Ramsbury, Marlborough
Wiltshire SN8 2HR

www.crowood.com

This impression 2007

© John Darling, 1996

All rights reserved. No part of this publication may be reproduced or transmitted in any form or by any means, electronic or mechanical, including photocopy, recording, or any information storage and retrieval system, without permission in writing from the publishers.

British Library Cataloguing in Publication Data

A catalogue record for this book is available from the British Library.

ISBN 978 1 85223 878 0

All photographs by John Darling.

Photograph page 2: Fighting a big bass on an Irish storm beach.

Typeset and designed by
D & N Publishing
Ramsbury, Marlborough
Wiltshire SN8 2HR

Typeface used: Galliard.

Phototypeset by HPS Ltd, Havant.

Printed and bound by CPI Bath

Contents

	Foreword *by Ron Preddy*	6
	Introduction	7
1	Biology and Physical Characteristics	9
2	Shore Fishing	27
3	Where to Find Bass Inshore	51
4	Reefs and Rocks	67
5	Baits	79
6	Boating for Bass	105
7	Fishing Offshore	119
8	Lures	133
9	Conservation and the Future for Bass	149
	Index	159

Foreword

This is a book for those who already love to catch big bass. It is also aimed at the less fortunate among us who have yet to catch such a fish, but would dearly love to. These two groups probably include every angler who has ever cast a line upon the sea.

Imagine the scene: dawn's first light reveals the dark curve of a carbon bass rod responding to the power of a silver-plated turbo-charged beauty beneath the waves. At long last, as if conceding defeat, the double-figure bass turns and glides majestically towards you, under the clear blue surface of a windless sea. The hookhold appears secure and the waiting net reaches out to secure the prize. For an instant, the eyes of the captured meet those of the captor. There is a brief pang of concern before the victor becomes aware that his specimen is safe. He cradles the beautiful fish in a manner befitting his own first-born, unable to believe his good fortune. The rush of adrenalin prevents him from putting a bait back into the water for some while. It is a magical experience that no word could properly express.

Big bass have become near-mythical creatures, but while accepting that they are extremely difficult to locate and catch, it must be said that the task is far from impossible. They vary their habitat according to instinct and opportunity. For every fish that cruises up-river under cover of darkness to wreak havoc in the shallows at first light, there are probably six more patrolling the weedy margins of a jagged reef just offshore. Seemingly programmed to avoid extinction, most big bass now favour the relative security provided by the thousands of shipwrecks dotted far out towards the beckoning horizon.

To catch quality fish from such a wide variety of angling opportunities takes an angler of the highest calibre. Those who make a study of such things realize that the specialists catch the vast majority of these fish. The author of this treatise, John Darling, is such an angler. He has written a highly informative book, revealing the amazing insights that he has accumulated in a lifetime's loving pursuit of a most demanding mistress. John and I have fished together for many years and have shared several outstanding catches of large bass. If, like me, you believe that big bass are the stuff of dreams and a worthy goal to strive for, then this book is for you.

Ron Preddy

Introduction

Catching bass is my passion. It occupies my thoughts for most of the summer and much of the winter, at any time of the day or night. Years ago a friend told me that if I spent as much time thinking about business as I spend thinking about *Dicentrachus labrax*, I would be a millionaire. I bet I would not have had as much fun as I have in more than thirty years of bass fishing. I have been writing about them for almost as long. My first article on the subject was published in *Creel* in May 1964. It was inspired by one of the most remarkable anglers of all time, a devout bass angler and one of the world's most gifted angling writers: Clive Gammon.

I owe a debt of gratitude to the many anglers who have given me snippets of information that have increased my understanding of bass and how to catch them. Some of these people are noted angling writers; others are anglers I have chatted to on the beach and around the harbour. Some old friends are now in that anglers' heaven where each bass is progressively larger and fights even harder, but they have to wait a tad longer for each one to strike.

Many anglers and boatmen have given me ideas to contemplate and tips to put into use. Some people have given me profound insights into bass behaviour, without realizing it. The tiniest scrap of information can be very valuable, particularly when it is the last piece of a jigsaw or confirmation of a suspicion.

Our hero, *Dicentrachus labrax*, the most sporting fish in British seas.

The bass is known throughout Europe, in various languages, as the 'sea wolf', or 'sea perch'. It is an exceedingly handsome, powerful fish, a total thug and a voracious predator. It gleams like a bar of precious metal and has a scorching turn of speed. Its power and aggression have caused it to be prized as one of the foremost game fish of the sea. For this reason, sport anglers hate commercial fishermen who have scant respect for their quarry, either alive or dead, and leave these noble fish to flap out their last gasps in the muck and grime at the bottom of a boat while they go about the business of catching more.

For shore anglers, bass are to be caught from some of the most awesome scenery anywhere. Whether they are running a rolling Atlantic surf on a wild storm beach where the

INTRODUCTION

mountains rise jagged against the sky, or striking baitfish behind a ledge that juts out beneath towering cliffs, bass anglers see coastal scenery at its best and all the spectacular shades of light and weather. As sunset fades, is there any better place to be in the world than on an immaculate, wild beach, with the breeze shrilling in a taut line and the savage, thumping strain against the rod of a nine-pounder?

Certain events mark the progress of a bass angler's addiction. When I was very young, I watched an angler pull in a six-pounder from a rocky cove. I was so impressed by its power, grace and beauty that I resolved to catch one myself. The first bass I handled was a two-and-a-half-pounder that I swapped for a whiting livebait with an angler who did not eat fish. The first bass I caught was a schoolie; the second one weighed 8¼lb. The third, the following night, weighed 10¼lb. "I've got it sussed", I thought but I rapidly discovered otherwise. As each new season dawns, I still feel I am starting on a fresh adventure.

Bass have brains and anybody who fails to remember that will catch very few. Bass are clever enough to avoid trammel nets in clear water, and to see through clumsy attempts to catch them on rod and line. Of course, they do daft things at times; but not often. The moment you start taking short cuts while hunting wild quarry, is when failure starts edging in.

You have to be single-minded and ignore sleep and tiredness to catch big bass. You have to clamber out of bed at ridiculous hours, heave rocks for crabs and expend a great deal of energy. Bass are caught most consistently by anglers who visit their marks frequently, who keep tabs on the fish's movements and who get a feel for the area that they fish. There are no fast tracks to success.

Catching big bass requires time, hard work, patience and attention to detail. Each season a fresh stratum of experience is laid down, and over the years you develop an instinct for where to find bass and how to coax them into accepting your offering.

That is only as it should be because bass are such wonderfully sporting fish. They have an awesome turn of speed which they use to kill mackerel or smash the line of the unwary angler. It is only right that anglers should serve an apprenticeship, so that they can develop their skills, and fully savour the moment when they have fought an enormous fish to a standstill and ultimately draw it into the landing net.

This book is not a basic angling primer. It assumes that a certain amount of knowledge has already been acquired. Neither can I state places to fish or where to find bait because that would make me very unpopular with a lot of anglers. Bass anglers are an odd lot, coming from all walks of life but united by a desire for the wild, unspoilt shorelines or the remote loneliness of a calm sea beyond the horizon. We share our secrets with our friends but hate it when strangers discover our marks. We owe thanks to people like Donovan Kelley, MBE, who has worked so hard in the interests of conservation. He undertook the painstaking research into bass long before anybody else took much interest. His findings have proved immensely valuable, especially with regard to the nursery areas.

This book is dedicated to every angler who feels that inner agitation when a warm breeze stirs the surf and sets the trees sighing and creaking, or when the sea is a glittering calm and the birds are pounding baitfish along the edge of a reef, or when dusk steals over the shore line as the tide laps lazily at the rocks and the line draws suddenly tight.

1 Biology and Physical Characteristics

PHYSICAL CHARACTERISTICS

Bass are almost impossible to confuse with any other European species of sea fish. Once seen, their appearance will never be forgotten. Their colour sometimes changes according to habitat. Although the belly is always silvery-white, the backs of bass caught over sand are often very pale, while those from reefs and offshore wrecks are usually very dark – almost black. This comes about because the fish can adapt their colour to blend into the background. Infant bass often have little black spots, which occasionally persist into adulthood. Very rarely, one encounters specimens with a yellowish hue over the back and flanks.

The shape of the head may sometimes vary, too. The head of most bass is usually pointed, but that of some is much more blunt. This foreshortened appearance makes them look as if they have received a punch on the nose at some time.

Anglers should beware that bass have a way of taking revenge on their captors, who should approach them with caution and handle them with care. An aggressive bass will raise its spiny dorsal fin and flare its gill cover to make two razor-sharp bony plates – the *opercula* – stand out. These plates can make nasty cuts on wet hands, and if a spine jabs you and the tip breaks off, the wound will linger for a long time.

DISTRIBUTION

Most bass fishing is practised to the south of a line imagined between Morecambe Bay and The Wash, though some are caught from the Solway Firth and the mouth of the River Luce on the west coast of Scotland. Some are caught in Yorkshire and a few have been taken

Plump winter bass like this prefer large baits anchored to the sea-bed.

BIOLOGY AND PHYSICAL CHARACTERISTICS

as far north as Aberdeen. In Ireland, most bass are found south of a line between the estuaries of the River Moy and River Boyne. Their range extends southwards as far as Morocco, and eastwards throughout the Mediterranean and the Black Sea.

Bass have been caught all round Scotland at one time or another, some large ones, but not in any abundance. This might be set to change with what some scientists are calling global warming. Fish from abundant year classes are caught all round the British Isles, as far as the north of Scotland. As adolescents, they range over a wide area and may restock some fished-out areas. Global warming may induce bass to over-winter farther east than normal, perhaps off Beachy Head and in the lower North Sea.

Bass happily forage for food in any depth of water from the fifty-metre line (as provided by marine charts) up to the inshore shallows. They will often hunt in water that is barely deep enough to cover their backs. They are also one of the few marine species adapted to living in brackish water and can even cope with river water that is bordering on fresh.

They are powerful swimmers, but that does not mean that they are particularly willing to ride strong currents. They find eddies and areas of slack water close by. They conserve energy for when (with powerful sweeps of the tail) they dash into the attack keeping every other fin flattened against the body. The main reason why bass strike spinners and plugs so violently is that they launch themselves like missiles at lures.

THE MOUTH

The bass's mouth is so large that it dwarfs big hooks. It is noted for being decidedly bony and lightly covered with a thick leathery skin that can be penetrated by only the sharpest of hooks. The outer part is like a pair of bellows. The maxillary jaws extend forwards, but are connected to the skull by only a thin membrane. The hook often lodges in this membrane, which tears slightly under pressure, forming a small hole. The bigger the fish and the harder it fights, the bigger the hole will be. All the fish needs is a bit of slack line as it lies on the surface, and it is likely to thrash around

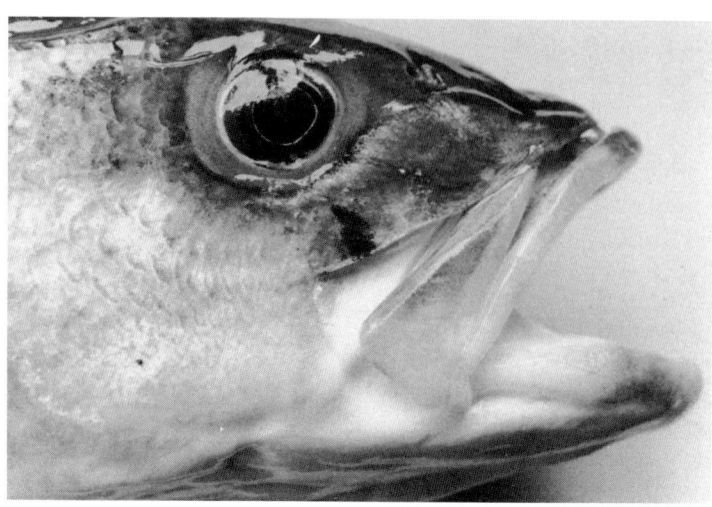

The large mouth and crushing jaws of bass make short work of baitfish.

BIOLOGY AND PHYSICAL CHARACTERISTICS

in every direction and throw the hook. I have seen it happen time and time again, particularly while landing fish from a boat.

In a moment's loss of concentration, while reaching for the landing net or watching your friend go to slide it under the fish, you forget to keep the line tight. In an instant, the bass thrashes its head and throws the hook. The fish sinks in the water then realizes it is free. With a few sweeps of its tail, it dives and disappears from sight.

Big bass can only be beaten with a bent rod and a tight line. It needs to be tight to the fish not the lead weight. That is how a friend of mine, who is new to bass fishing, lost an eleven-pounder last summer. It was a memorable fish, not least because we were fishing a local specimen competition. It would have cleaned up a lot of prizes.

SENSORY PERCEPTION

Bass have excellent eyesight. Their large, expressionful eyes cover 360 degrees, and are very quick to spot potential prey and assist them to catch it at lightning speed. They have little trouble seeing anglers moving against the skyline. It is advisable to keep low or out of sight when fishing clear shallow water, as though you are fishing a stream for chub.

At night it is most unwise to use a light that shines over the water. Although bass use bright lighting to silhouette their prey, I doubt if they are attracted to lights for any other reason. The flash caused by a torch shone out onto the water, or by somebody walking near a Tilley lamp, is likely to frighten them. They often swim close to the angler's feet at night, and a misdirected beam of light at the wrong moment might make all the difference between a successful trip and a blank. Even when landing fish, it is wise to keep the lights off. Use whatever is coming

A fifteen pounder, caught by a specialist bass angler.

from the night sky when directing a fish into the net.

Bass have frequently shown that they spend a lot of time in a small area, so it is quite possible that they take a dim view of finding a bright light where none should be. Most night bassmen carry a small torch or headlamp and only turn it on when they are facing away from the sea. On a big beach, a pressure lamp at a base camp above the highwater mark is acceptable, provided that it is a long way from the fishing area.

The bass's senses of taste and smell are highly developed, and it may use them to map

11

BIOLOGY AND PHYSICAL CHARACTERISTICS

migration routes. It is certainly very good for locating big, juicy baits of squid, mackerel and crab, but they do need to be big and juicy. Because bass feed more by sight, their sense of smell is not as good as that of an eel or a dogfish.

Nobody really knows precisely what vibrations bass pick up on their lateral line, but their sonar system certainly enables them to swim around in rough, murky conditions at night without any trouble at all. Under these conditions, bass rule the roost in European waters because they are safe from sharks, seals, porpoises and nearly every other predator, except man. During the day, it is possible that the bass are summoned to dense masses of baitfish by the sound of mackerel, bass, garfish and other predators striking the fish, by the sound of baitfish as they endeavour to escape, and by the sound of splashing, dive-bombing sea birds.

The bigger the fish, the bigger the swim bladder, and the more it resonates with underwater vibrations (and the better it shows up on the fish finder). These vibes are fed to the inner ear by a chain of small bones. The implication is that bass can 'hear' better as they get older and wiser, so they are increasingly likely to be more scared of the noise of sport-fishing boats

Nowadays bass rarely tolerate boats whizzing around them unless they are in a feeding frenzy. Sometimes anglers are too keen to catch them. Just when the birds are starting to work, somebody goes charging through them in his boat, anxious to begin a drift. The fish go down, the birds drift away and another golden opportunity is scuppered by ignorance.

In common with cod, bass are circumspect of an anchored boat. In calm water, you can

Rock ledges like this enable bass to be caught by a wide variety of methods.

12

BIOLOGY AND PHYSICAL CHARACTERISTICS

easily see the wave of disturbance that the hull sends out to each side and this seems to disturb the fish. They also dislike the vibrations coming from the anchor rope. If you imagine the boat as a soundboard, as on a guitar, and the anchor rope as a single string, it is easy to appreciate that the presence of a boat can disturb the bass.

For this reason up-tide casting is widely practised, casting baits away from the hull and out of the zone of disturbance. When riding at anchor in a small GRP bass boat and fishing with rods in rests, the tide acting on the line causes it to sing in an eerie manner, like the singing of distant whales or an old woman humming. It sounds quite loud on calm days, but it does not seem to upset the fish.

HABITAT

People and boats are most active during the day, and for this reason many harbours and estuaries are devoid of bass of any decent size by day. However, such places are good larders, full of small fish and crustaceans, and the bass know it. They visit under cover of darkness, coming in with the tide when everything is quiet. At high water around two o'clock in the morning is a good tide for these bass.

Bass feel more secure and feed throughout the day in deep water, offshore – 75–100ft (23–30m). While in shallow water inshore – 20–30ft (6–9m) – they may be disturbed by bathers, li-los, surf-boards, jet-skis, boats, water-skiers, ferries, nets, and other unnatural goings-on. Unless the shoreline is rarely disturbed, I suspect that some bass hole up during the day in deep gullies among reefs, inside wrecks and within the structure of seaside piers (the ones that stand on stilts). The exception to this general rule is when baitfish are around. Bass refuges are also baitfish refuges, and although the bass may not be hunting very actively, they are unlikely to pass up an easy meal.

In many areas, inshore fishing with bait is generally more successful shortly after dawn or as dusk comes in, but a lot of good bass have been caught on plugs and spinners within a short distance of the edge during bright, calm, sunny conditions. I have also caught them from the rocks on crab under similar circumstances. On a few occasions I have caught them from the surf in bright, sunny weather. However, bass do appear to have become more circumspect about their daytime activities over the years. This, fortunately, permits anglers to ambush them when they leave their lairs at dusk.

Night fishing in autumn, with a large squid bait just beyond the waves.

13

BIOLOGY AND PHYSICAL CHARACTERISTICS

Bass that are large enough to interest anglers can be found in a wide variety of habitats: seething surf, tide-races, rocky bays and headlands, around sandbanks, reefs, wrecks and inside estuaries where they penetrate upstream to where the water is brackish. Each of these different areas will be dealt with in greater detail in a later chapter, but they all share one factor in common: they are places where bass can find their prey at a disadvantage.

Bass shelter from raging spring tides in large estuaries, in harbours, around large reefs and the largest wrecks. They do not relish very rough seas, big swells or heavy undertows. I have caught more bass in calm seas and gentle surfs than I ever have in rough weather, other than by seeking out sheltered corners. Middling tides and more gentle conditions generally produce the best catches. Local knowledge should be heeded, but some local habits may have grown out of laziness rather than perspicacity. Bass are often caught by anglers who ignore local knowledge and follow their own instincts.

Bass will tolerate a wide variety of temperatures, but prefer water around 10–20°C (50–68°F). Fish in estuaries and shallow water move to slightly deeper more comfortable water when the air temperature drops sharply, and they are attracted into sun-warmed shallows, particularly early in the season when the sea is still warming up. It is well known that bass are attracted to warm-water outfalls, like those from power stations and industrial cooling plants. These warm outlets are favoured by juvenile bass, which often spend the entire winter close by them. In autumn, as the sea cools, adult fish migrate to deeper water, down to 260ft (80m) off the south-west of England, where the temperature is more constant, and they spend the winter there.

Algal blooms are a problem. Unfortunately it seems that theses are being encouraged

Rustington Beach, 1950: my first ever crabbing expedition.

these days by the amount of pulverized sewage that is being pumped into the sea. Algal blooms reduce oxygen levels considerably and are absolutely no good for bass fishing. The bloom eventually sinks. Divers tell me that the sea can look clear on top, but down below there is a thick layer of algae which blocks out the light.

MIGRATION

A few tagged fish have been found to travel large distances in a short time, suggesting that they swim quite fast while migrating, possibly 20 miles (30km) or more in a day and 150 miles (240km) in a week. Tagging has shown that some fish cross the Western Approaches between England and the coast of France, although it is no longer believed that there is a mass migration of what used to be referred to as 'Biscay bass'. There appears to be no mixing of Irish and British stocks, suggesting that they do not migrate across the Irish Sea. They are rarely found more than 50 miles (80km) offshore but have been trawled up from 180ft (55m).

Many species of fish migrate by making use of tidal currents. This is called 'selected tidal

BIOLOGY AND PHYSICAL CHARACTERISTICS

stream transport'. The fish use the tide to carry them over towards their destination. When the tide changes and the current reverses its direction, they hunker down, get into shelter, rest and sometimes feed, while waiting for the tide to turn again.

When migrating, bass often form very large shoals offshore. Each May two or three vast shoals appear off Beachy Head in Sussex. These shoals can sometimes be up to a mile (1.6km) long, and are believed to be everybody else's bass migrating up-Channel to Kent, the Thames Estuary, the North Sea and beyond. While migrating, the fish are generally to be found at one or two well-known marks for a day, with only a few stragglers remaining the following day. They appear to migrate under cover of darkness.

Years ago huge shoals like this could sometimes be seen close to shore, and seine netters working from beaches like Pendine in Glamorgan and some Cornish and Sussex beaches made large catches, sometimes of very big fish, but not any more. Nowadays trawlers working in pairs look for groups of bass boats on their radar and plough into the shoal.

Tagging has shown that most bass are remarkably faithful to their migration routes. The majority of fish that are tagged in a specific area are caught in the same area, within 20 miles (30km), over succeeding years. However, some fish have been recaptured hundreds of miles from their tagging site. One from the Thames Estuary was recaptured on the north coast of Spain after a journey of about 600 miles (950km).

Little can be deduced from this. It might have been a fish from Biscay that travelled north to feed (a journey it could achieve in little over a fortnight); it might have originated

When the sea pinks come into bloom, the crabs are peeling and the bass return to the reefs.

15

BIOLOGY AND PHYSICAL CHARACTERISTICS

Casting into a gentle surf on Inch Strand, Co. Kerry. Bass now receive some measure of protection in Ireland.

BIOLOGY AND PHYSICAL CHARACTERISTICS

in Brittany; it could have been an English bass. Maybe it had developed a taste for young tuna, which would be in keeping with the bass's buccaneering spirit. In the end, evidence points to the fact that most bass stick to the same migration route year after year once they mature.

After spending four to five years of their childhood exploring a particular patch of territory, it is not surprising that bass return to it in each successive migration. This bodes ill for conservation. If bass stocks are wiped out through overfishing in a specific area, there is little chance of mass recruitment from outside areas. Bassmen everywhere can testify to an overwhelming pile of evidence to show that this has happened, and is still happening, around the British Isles. Other species, particularly birds, return to the same square yard where they were hatched after spending months at sea, circumnavigating the world. Many wild creatures memorize maps of where they live. Woodpigeons, for example, spend two months showing their young around their home patch so that they memorize the landmarks. We have yet to discover precisely what steers bass around the unimaginably huge expanses of sea – magnetite perhaps, in the pores of the lateral line, like salmon, or perhaps they recognize the characteristic smell of their home range.

The movement of bass around the British Isles is understood well enough, from the angler's point of view. In general terms, the first bass of the year can be expected in late February in Cornwall, and in the West Country and the Channel Islands in March. April sees the first fish in Sussex and the Thames Estuary, but for most of us it is May before catches become reliable. In June and July bass are everywhere, on into August, September and October. Some are caught in November and occasionally in December, further west. They are caught in December in Ireland where the Gulf Stream brushes the shore, although the best times for the Kerry surf beaches are January to June and then again in the autumn.

As a general rule, bass from the North Sea and the English Channel drift south and west in October, November and December, while those along the west coast drift south. The bass around Cornwall seem to hang around the vicinity throughout the year. The migration would appear to start earlier on the west coast, in September. By January, bass are somewhere in the mild Atlantic between Cornwall and Brittany.

Years ago my friends and I used to catch the occasional 7–10lb bass around Christmas and early in the New Year from beaches in Sussex, which suggests that some fish might have been over-wintering in deeper water farther from shore. Most juvenile bass keep to within 30 miles (50km) of their home patch, but a few juvenile and adolescent bass yearn for the open road, as befits a species with a buccaneering temperament. They roam miles from home, particularly as they approach maturity. Big bass range farther as they grow older. Fish from the Thames Estuary and Anglesey have to travel in excess of 300 miles (480km) to their over-wintering area, and back again the next year. Some 12–15lb bass will have wandered thousands of miles during their lifetime.

The bass start to move north and east from their over-wintering areas in February, spawning as they go, but anglers don't encounter meaningful shoals until May, when the fish have all but completed spawning and the water has warmed up sufficiently to induce feeding. This is when the scales first show signs of new-season growth. By mid-summer, nearly all of the bass will have returned to the same area that was to their liking the previous season. This naturally separates British bass into fairly specific groups.

17

BIOLOGY AND PHYSICAL CHARACTERISTICS

PREY AND FEEDING

Bass are opportunists and readily exploit any source of food that comes their way. They are not above taking food waste that is thrown overboard from ships or is dumped from restaurants on piers, where they can be caught on balls of cheese paste. Years ago a Newhaven angler used to thread baked beans up his hook and onto the line, and free-line this offering among the slops that were thrown overboard from cross-Channel ferries. Bass regularly visit harbours and estuaries where fish waste is dumped overboard by netsmen.

A friend of mine, Digger Derrington, once caught a bass from a sewer outfall. It contained a drowned mouse. He set some traps in his garden shed, caught some mice, and ended up catching a 4lb bass on one of them Other friends have caught bass containing a packet of kippers (with its plastic wrapper intact), and a packet of cheese (also complete with its plastic packaging). This surely says something about the sensitivity of the bass's sense of smell. They have been found with chicken bones inside them, and one perfectly healthy specimen was caught with a meat skewer sticking out of its flank. In time, it would probably have passed right through and the wound would have healed. After all, it is not uncommon to find boa constrictors with the horns of their prey sticking out of one side. Bass are often caught in crab and lobster pots, which they have entered, intent on filching the bait.

Inshore, bass tend to hunt in loose gangs, moving quite rapidly through an area and on to the next likely larder. I have seen shoals foraging over the sea-bed with their heads down, hunting for crabs, molluscs, fish, worms and anything else that looks edible. When they find shoals of baitfish, they set about them with a vengeance, driving them upwards and away from cover. These attacks are usually related to some sort of structure on the sea-bed, where the bass wait in ambush, and where the tidal currents put the baitfish at a disadvantage. They are usually picked off individually, but when the bass are numerous and so are the baitfish, I think that the bass drive into the shoals to stun them.

On several occasions while fishing in my boat over large shoals of feeding bass, I have observed dead sprats drifting away with the tide some 20ft (6m) below the surface. In calm conditions, the bass can be seen swirling at the surface, until some boat ploughs through and puts them off the feed. Years ago the shoals of bass were so thick off some parts of Britain that you could drive through them at full speed and still catch fish.

I once saw seventeen boats off Beachy Head complete the drift together when I was just starting. It looked for all the world like a powerboat race coming towards me. Often I have been drifting through a shoal of bass, with the gulls screaming and diving all around me, and have seen a sprat go dashing away just under the surface, throwing out a wake like a miniature torpedo. A gull has dived onto the fish, but a bass has got there first, and the desperate baitfish has disappeared amid a heavy swirl. By that time, my rod was usually locked over and bucking to a wildly fighting eight-pounder – or I would anxiously be wondering why it wasn't.

Even in quite deep water – 100ft (30m) for example – the bass drive the bait upwards, and very often the seagulls can see the action going on beneath them. The bass go into a feeding frenzy, which is matched by the gulls. No other sight gladdens the heart of a bass angler more than that of a plume of seagulls, their white wings flickering in the early morning sunlight, working over a shoal of feeding bass – unless they are miles out of casting range. A feeding frenzy acts like a magnet to all other fish around.

BIOLOGY AND PHYSICAL CHARACTERISTICS

Diving gulls often reveal where fish are feeding.

Years ago I anchored up very close in on a reef. I was fishing with some perfect crab bait, and I saw three other boats whizzing around a couple of miles farther out. The weather was blindingly bright, so I should have been spinning instead. As if to tell me that they were hunting for fish, two large bass swam up and closely inspected the dimples where my line entered the water. The boats offshore loaded up, but the fish were also close in and were on the lookout for prey.

Structure – wrecks, reefs and sandbanks – is not always essential. Sometimes bass find a shoal of baitfish on open ground, far from cover. Opportunities like this are more frequent than some anglers realize. The birds look as if they are working over mackerel shoals, but bass are beneath them.

The speed with which a bass attacks its prey can be awesome, particularly when you are fishing with livebait. For this reason, I don't wait around much if takes are slow in coming. If the fish are there, I usually get an offer within minutes of casting out or dropping a bait down to them. I have often hooked bass within seconds of presenting my bait. When this is the first fish of the day, it usually foretells a hectic session. Unless the water conditions change, a lot more fish are likely to be down there waiting for the bait.

From the shore, however, you have to wait for the fish to move with the tide and be influenced by the much more changeable sea conditions that are found around the edges of the ocean. None the less, a similar sort of certainty can be expected from the shore. In many places, at a specific hour in the tide, the bass may come past and be willing to feed. Success at any method of bass fishing requires careful calculations and some input from the bass. They may not be obliging on seven trips out of ten, but those three successful sessions can be relied on to refuel your enthusiasm for at least another season.

The speed with which bass take is relative to the size of the shoal and the amount of competition among the individual fish, but it should also be noted that when there is little competition, as when fishing with crab inshore, the takes can be very slow. Under these conditions, the only indication that a bass is at the bait may be a light drawing on the line, or a slight tap such as a crab would give. Almost always, these gentle takes occur close to shore and where the current is negligible. I was taught very early in my bassing career that

19

unless I could recognize these offers, I might miss the opportunity of the day. I have watched the rod-tip of inexperienced bassmen and have seen bass gently move it without the angler realizing that he has just had an offer. Having said that, a friend of mine was out in my boat on one of his first ever fishing expeditions, and his rod was dragged the full length of the cockpit. The only thing that saved it from being lost overboard was the reel, which jammed against a cleat at the stern. He turned to me, his eyes full of innocence, and asked, 'Was that a bite?'.

One advantage of living in a shoal is that experiences can be shared. It often seems that every bass in a shoal is aware of what its colleagues are up to. This is most dramatically illustrated when a large, rampaging gang of bass is found feeding on baitfish and one is hooked. After the main part of the fight, as the fish is being drawn towards the bait, you might see that the rest of the shoal has followed the hooked fish. Sometimes it is hard to pick out which one is hooked because there are so many dark shapes swimming behind it. More often than not, the one with the bait is dwarfed by the fish swimming alongside it, some of them well into double figures.

This can be turned to advantage by flicking a spinner or other lure in front of the ones that have swum up to see what is happening. The twisting and turning of a hooked bass looks as if it is snapping individuals out of a shoal of baitfish. The others, keen to get in on the act, are naturally curious. Like mackerel, they can then be caught by the stringful.

However, I once found a school of tiny bass fry beside my boat and crumbled some bread into fine pieces to see if they would take. One of the basslings at the head of the shoal darted up, grabbed a crumb, tasted it, then spat it out. Another fish, farther back in in the school, went up and inspected the crumb from a distance of about an inch (2.5cm), dropping back with the current as it did so. Then it turned away and resumed its original position. After that the entire shoal completely ignored the breadcrumbs. At the time, it was getting towards low tide, and the barnacle-encrusted rails of a ladder had become exposed. I used the back of a knife to scrape off some barnacles, mashed them up and tempted the basslings once again. Recognizing the smell of blood (rather than yeast) they all piled in and gulped down the tiny scraps of meat.

A few days later, in Newhaven Marina, I found a freshwater outflow that drains into the river. It was high summer, and the flow of water was negligible, but I saw a few bass fry down there and decided to try an experiment. I popped into the Harbour Tackle Shop, where Dennis O'Kennedy donated a razor-fish to a good cause.

I shelled the razor-fish, then pulverized it and fed it into the water outlet. Within seconds, the bass fry were crowding round, and I whipped them into such a frenzy with the mashed razor-fish that it looked as if I had sprinkled silver Christmas glitter into the outfall. One of the advantages of feeding at speed is that the bass can get a lot down their gullet quickly.

When bass are hungry, they eat lots. They may go after a large number of individual items, like crabs or even tiny slaters and sand-hoppers, but sometimes they prefer to attack the biggest items of prey that won't attack them first. Bass are frequently caught from estuaries, their stomachs hard and tight with shore crabs. One seven-pounder that I caught from the rocks had three 6in (15cm) wide soft edible crabs inside it. I have frequently caught bass on very large live and dead baits. Sometimes I catch bass that are not much longer than the livebait that they have just killed. A 1lb bass will readily attack an 8in (20cm) joey mackerel if it looks weak enough to catch.

I have witnessed several encounters between bass fry and the fry of other species,

BIOLOGY AND PHYSICAL CHARACTERISTICS

Mackerel boiling on the surface may not be attacking fry but escaping from a shoal of lunker bass.

and they usually end up with a little tail protruding from the bass's mouth. Why not? The fish can still breathe easily through its gills, and it won't feel hungry again until it has emptied its mouth. It makes great sense. Throughout the season, bass of all sizes can usually be found attending concentrations of baitfish.

A few seasons back I witnessed an awe-inspiring attack by a big bass. A chum and I were drifting a wreck, and I had just boated a ten-pounder on a mackerel weighing about 1½lbs. Bait was very scarce, and it was the only one we had caught. I decided to live dangerously, dropped the feathers down to the wreck, and hauled up a pollack of nearly 3lbs. It looked much too big, but I decided to put it on for bait, on my friend's rod. Half-way through the drift, the rod was dragged into a hoop by a savagely powerful take. The bass dived into the wreck, despite my mate having both thumbs hard down on the spool of the reel. The line snagged as the rod hit maximum curve. First the rod snapped and then the line. That was some bass - at least 15lbs.

Bass of all ages prey on a wide variety of fish and crustaceans. Most of the time they feed on items that are locally abundant. For example, bass feeding inshore will eat shrimps, shore crabs and worms, while those offshore feed mainly on fish, although they are not above taking masked crabs when baitfish are scarce. Much of the characteristic behaviour of large bass can be found among fry. You can see this by observing where shoals of bassling station themselves while feeding and in their manner of attacking prey. Baby bass feed primarily on zooplankton, tiny crustaceans, and fry, but as they grow they increasingly prey on small fish and larger crustaceans, like crabs. Not all the bass in a shoal feed at the same time. Some are found to be full of food, while others are completely empty.

21

BIOLOGY AND PHYSICAL CHARACTERISTICS

Local availability is the key when considering the prey of bass, particularly offshore. During the summer months, sprats, sandeels and mackerel are most frequently consumed. In autumn, when the baitfish fry of the year have reached a reasonable size and mackerel are becoming scarce, the bass feed on scad, whiting, pouting, and poor cod. However, I am inclined to believe that bass become less aggressive in the autumn. After two months of hard feeding in June and July, their bodies are packed with fat and they become lazy about chasing baitfish. Nowadays most of my fishing in July is directed at the shoals of big fish offshore. Often the bass feed all day. They seem to stop chasing baitfish as darkness falls and start again at dawn.

In early July, sunrise is at 4.45 a.m., and sunset is at 9.15 p.m. The bass have more than seventeen hours of daylight and three tides in which to hunt out large items of prey like pouting, sprats, launce, mackerel, scad and pollack. It is hardly any wonder that they pack on so much weight and become so fat during this period. The first fish that I catch in June are generally slim and are known locally as 'racers'. By the end of July, many of them will have increased their body weight by ten to fifteen per cent. This is unsurprising because bass of both sexes feed up after spawning, although it seems that they slow down once they have rebuilt their reserves of body fat.

Inshore bass sometimes feed extensively on ragworms when they leave their burrows to spawn in the spring. They form thick clouds in some places. Any bass that happens upon one of these congregations is unlikely to pass up on such a bonanza.

Shoaling bass are suicidal when in a feeding frenzy.

BIOLOGY AND PHYSICAL CHARACTERISTICS

SPAWNING

When the sea temperature is around 10°C (50°F), spawning begins in mid-February off the west coast of Britain and continues through March and into June along the south coast. February, March and April are the peak months. Off Sussex, I can catch a lot of large male bass in July that liberally squirt me with milt. Whether or not these fish are still spawning at that time, I am unable to say. However, once the sea temperature reaches 15°C (59°F), very few bass eggs turn up in plankton trawls. At this temperature, the fry are likely to be born deformed.

Bass do not shed all their eggs at once. The gonads mature gradually, so it should be possible for a female to lay some eggs in the Bristol Channel, another load off the Eddystone, some more off Beachy Head, and complete her season's procreation in the Thames Estuary. Bass shed their spawn in mid-water, far from land, and the eggs and larvae have been found covering a wide area and at all depths. Because of this, it is very hard to pinpoint precise spawning areas. However, they are not around headlands and estuaries, as was once thought. Because bass spawn over a fairly long period, it is not uncommon to find shoals of fry that are larger or smaller than each other. This disparity in size sometimes leads to cannibalism, with the earlier larger fry taking some of the smaller ones.

The eggs hatch about a week after fertilization, depending on the temperature. They hatch twice as quickly at 15°C (59°F) as at 10°C (50°F). The larvae make their way inshore, although how they do it is unknown. They take eight to twelve weeks to find the coast line, and by June the first fry of the season are found in sheltered marinas, harbours, tidal pools, estuaries, and marshland creeks, often in brackish water, where large shoals sometimes congregate. Here the bass stay,

The bass was caught on peeler spider crab; the rabbit was found injured on the bank of an estuary.

Feeding slows considerably once the sea temperature ducks below 10°C (50°F). The cooler the water, the longer it takes bass to digest their food. Conversely, the higher the sea temperature, the faster the chemical reactions in a bass's stomach and the greater the amount of food it can consume and process into body weight.

BIOLOGY AND PHYSICAL CHARACTERISTICS

Autumn is the best time to catch large, plump bass – like this one from Dungeness.

migrating only a short distance offshore during the winter months. They spend the next four to five years living in these sheltered nursery areas, returning to the same place each summer. When they are four years old and reaching maturity, they become more adventurous and move to deeper water, joining the adult stock.

Following legislation in 1990, thirty-four of the most important nursery areas were awarded official protection, where fishing and netting are prohibited. These nurseries contain large numbers of the tiny crustaceans, especially shrimp-like creatures called mysids, that baby bass eat. They offer higher water temperatures than those found in the open sea and, of course, the fry are less exposed to small inshore predators like mackerel, pollack, coalfish, scad and garfish.

Baby bass over-winter close to shore and in the channels of larger estuaries. They can therefore be caught out by a prolonged cold spell, which can weaken them, make them less able to fend for themselves and may even kill them. An entire year class can be wiped out by a severe winter, which is one reason why global warming, if it happens, may benefit bass stocks. Since bass don't feed in cold seas, they have to rely on the reserves of fat that were laid down the previous summer. A prolonged freeze-up taxes their strength. The weakest die, but the bigger, fatter basslings are likely to survive. A warm, settled summer provides bass fry with abundant feeding and a mild winter ensures their survival to the next year. These two factors govern the success of any particular year class.

Bass are sensitive to water temperature. They come in to feed when the tide rises over a foreshore that has been warmed by the sun during the day and move into the warmer water along the shore line. If the tide floods over a foreshore that has been chilled by inclement weather, the bass stay out where the water is warmer. Baby bass respond to these different weather conditions in like manner.

GROWTH

Fish mature at length, not age. Bass live for twenty years or more, growing wiser all the time. There is a strong correlation between high water temperatures and increased growth among both fry and adult bass. The warmer and more settled the spring and

BIOLOGY AND PHYSICAL CHARACTERISTICS

Not ideal conditions for bass fishing, but you never know when a fifteen pounder will turn up.

summer, the higher the survival rate for basslings and the faster they grow. This can lead to such strong year classes that these fish dominate catches over subsequent years.

When bass are large enough to start spawning and migrating between summer feeding areas and over-wintering areas, they are considered to be mature. The majority of bass mature at 16in (42cm), and fish under 3lbs are known as school bass or 'schoolies'. Male bass do not grow as large as females and take longer. The females can usually be identified only when they are gutted. They have orange-pink roes, with tiny eggs visible. Males have whitish-grey roes and may squirt you with milt. This is extremely slippery, so it should always be mopped up from the floor of the boat after landing a large, vigorous male.

Bass grow from late May to October. Growth ceases in winter and when spawning in spring. Males grow much more slowly than females, which have to grow large in order to hold bulky eggs. A 10lb female might contain in excess of two million eggs. Bass become very fat by September and stay like this until February. Their gonads start to grow in November and are at their largest in March and April. The preparation for spawning absorbs most of this fat, and the spent fish look very lean in May, when the cycle of feeding begins again.

Water temperature is the main factor governing the growth rate of bass. Fish along the south-east coast are the fastest growing in the British Isles. More double-figure bass are caught between Suffolk and Dorset than from the rest of Britain put together. This is to be expected because the bass that swim our seas are at the northern extreme of their range. They grow considerably faster in Morocco but die younger.

BIOLOGY AND PHYSICAL CHARACTERISTICS

This twelve-pounder did its best to drag my friend out of the boat. The one I hooked on the same drift fought back into the wreck and smashed my tackle.

The growth rate of any fish can be read in the rings (the *annuli*) of the scales, like reading the age of a tree. It can also be read from the flat bones in the gill-cover (the *opercula*). Bass have large scales, which assist reading their age. The best scales are those from the middle of the flank, but some scales may have been replaced due to loss through injury, in which case they do not hold a full record of the fish's growth. A scale's outer edge shows the current season's growth.

Some two dozen bass over 17lbs have been caught by anglers since 1945. Commercial fishermen have netted considerably more and bigger. Both the current record fish, from boat and shore, are mere ounces apart, at over 19lbs, which proves that very large bass are as likely to be caught close in as far offshore, although they are more numerous out there. Two friends of mine caught five over 14lbs in three days one autumn.

The maximum size a bass is likely ever to achieve is 25lb and 40in (100cm). Very large bass are females. They are also heavier for their length than males. That is why I would rather catch a female. When bass reach maturity, growth slows with the onset of spawning, then increases again. A mature fish may put on a pound or more each year for the rest of its life. The larger it grows, the more powerful it becomes, enabling it to catch and swallow bigger meals, which is exactly what bass are perfectly equipped to do.

2 Shore Fishing

My career as a bass fisherman began in 1962, although my biggest prize that year was a pouting of about a pound. I saw people catching bass – schoolies mainly – and I had already been deeply struck by the beauty of bass at that tender age, so I considered myself a bass angler, albeit an unsuccessful one.

Like most novices, I stared along the shore line and let my eyes wander out to the horizon. Both horizon and shore line seemed to go on forever, with a vast expanse of sea in between. I realized that I didn't have the first clue about what I was supposed to be looking for, nor even how to recognize a clue if it was perched on a rock in front of me. It seemed impossible to understand what the sea-bed was like out there, where the bass might be, and when I should go fishing for them.

Failure attends a large part of our early efforts in any sport. It is inevitable, and provided we do not waste emotion on feeling angry, helpless and humiliated, some wisdom can usually be salvaged from even the worst disaster. A Chinese proverb ends with the words '...if you want to be happy for life, learn to fish', and I believe that bass fishing is a life-long experience. Year after year, season after season, the accretion of experience gradually pays dividends. Some of these lessons are painful, like the monster fish that throws the hook and escapes, but often they are highly delightful.

A few seasons after I started bass fishing, I spent a lot of time scurrying around the British Isles fishing different areas, many of which were renowned for producing half a dozen good fish on a reasonable tide. Some of these trips paid off and decent bass were landed, but most of the time the wind and

Seaford Head: bass country where I learned my craft.

SHORE FISHING

How not to catch bass: a fish could heave the rod over and reject the bait before this angler could put down his mug of tea.

weather worked against success and I returned home skunked. All those expeditions added to my experience in some way.

I came to realize that my journeys around Britain were not particularly necessary as more than enough bass could be found around my home patch, so I set about exploring my own backyard and meeting the local bass fishermen, like Graham Roberts. Sport became considerably more consistent.

To be successful as a beach angler, you have to think in five dimensions. The first aspect to consider is the nature of the foreshore and the bass attracting ground immediately offshore. The second is the height of the tide and the strength of the current, on the flood or the ebb. The third is the weather, including the temperature, wind speed and direction, and whether there is sunshine or cloud cover. The fourth is the time of day or night. The fifth is the time of year. Thankfully, many of these combinations are generally well-understood in bass fishing areas, and the anglers know where to go, when, and how to tackle each situation. Sometimes, tide, time and wind come together with such immaculate precision that every nerve in your body is screaming 'Get down there'.

There is no greater high for a shore fisherman than to be standing in the surf, feeling the tide surging against his waders, listening to the breaking waves. Many times I have stood there, waiting for that sudden snatch as an eight-pounder pounces on my peeler crab and moves away fast, looking for the next one. When a shoal is working the shore line, there

SHORE FISHING

is little time for manners. They travel fast, with their heads down like a pack of hounds spread out along the surf line.

In the growing darkness, you switch into automatic mode, letting the rod-tip answer the rhythm of the surf plucking at the line as your eyes wander over the dark gloom of the land. Distant pin-pricks of light pick out the farms on the far hill, but the clouds are too thick for stars. The take, when it comes, jolts everything back into focus. There's a sudden twitch on the line, quite out of phase with the surf, generally followed by a savage pull. It is a wonderful experience. Then there is the uncertainty of the fight, the first sighting as the fish thrashes in the shallows and that perfect moment when it slides safely up the beach and the waves recede from it.

There are certain classic occasions in all types of bass fishing when everything comes together perfectly, and I have been fortunate to enjoy many of them. They can all provide the angler with thrilling sport and a day to remember. The successful combination of place, tide, weather, season and time of day, it isn't too hard to establish your own formula for different marks. This can lead to serious clashes of loyalties when conditions perfect for fishing coincide with social or business commitments. Surely man was born to fish, not to commute?

As you get older and become more shrewd and mean, you learn not to waste good bass fishing time, even when friends and family are getting married or dropping dead all around. Comes the tide, comes forth the angler, and the only way to catch bass consistently is by answering the call of the tide at any time of the day or night. Because bass have a fairly exact notion of how much energy to expend in pursuit of food and the sea conditions they find favourable, they tend to operate within a fairly narrow band of tide and weather conditions. This in turn makes their habits fairly

Feeling for that first tap in wild Welsh surf.

predictable. Once you suss out what they are up to in any given location, you can rely on the formula working more often than not. The trouble is getting the formula right, and not making the wrong assumptions about what influences the behaviour of the fish.

A classic example of this is how the shore fishing picks up in many areas during spring tides. Like many other anglers, I used to think this was because bass like strong tides. I now think that the inshore stock of fish is increased by bass moving inshore to shelter from the full force of the current. They may have come from wrecks, reefs and ledges that offer insubstantial protection against a big spring tide. Once the currents have eased up again and the tides shorten down to neaps, the bass resume their roaming.

Another example is that we used to think that bass did not feed by day in bright, calm, clear conditions, but of course they do. They

SHORE FISHING

Casting out a peeler, using a spark plug as a sinker. Fancy tackle is not necessary to catch bass.

go hunting fish in the tide-races, and a large shoal may be within casting range of the beach, but the fish have absolutely no interest in anything lying dead on the sea-bed. They are looking for sprats, sandeels, scad, pouting, whiting, joey mackerel, small pollack, and poor cod – anything that moves that they can scrunch between their jaws.

Even when inshore, they prefer to operate where the current is temperate. I often fish a long ledge that is gradually submerged by the rising tide. As the current increases in strength and the water deepens, the bass move closer and closer to the shore to escape its full force. By fishing from my boat, up-anchoring, and dropping the hook again 50yds (46m) closer to land, I have been able to catch up with the fish again after an unproductive spell further out. When the bass move even closer to land, I up-anchor and move again. On many occasions I have caught more fish closer in than I ever used to catch while casting from the rocks. This is because I was unaware of precisely what the bass were up to and failed to read a pattern in their behaviour. Had I been more experienced, I would have known how to change my tactics, shorten my casts and start catching again.

However, this is the angler's scourge. Trying to read rhyme and reason into the behaviour of fish can make it very easy to overlook certain factors. The fish adapt their

SHORE FISHING

behaviour, but the angler does not adapt because he fails to recognize the opportunities around him. He ceases fishing because he believes that the fish have ceased feeding, but they haven't. I can think of several occasions when the prospect of a tremendous day's sport was right under my nose, but I failed to sniff it out and seize the chance. It seems that in this game one's eyes are forever being opened wider and wider.

I remember an occasion one autumn when the sea was full of sprats, mackerel and a host of other tiddlers. I was silently drifting in my boat over a series of rock ledges and large boulders that were too high up the tide line to be of much interest even to the crabs. My echo-sounder showed large bass lurking around these ledges and boulders, waiting for baitfish to come to them on the current. The water was so shallow that I was fearful of clonking the propeller on a rock, but I now know another good place to try a spot of plug fishing – from the shore.

Bass are found in such a variety of places that they can never be pinned down completely. Every year anglers play hunches which may go against the grain of received wisdom, and sometimes they get a wonderful surprise. I'm not saying that we should all fish like the holiday-maker who drops a half-rotten squid over the side of a pier and hauls in a twelve-pounder, but it is sometimes easy to look too hard at the tide chart, worry too much about the weather, and argue yourself out of going fishing. You should never lose sight of the fact that bass are close to the coast of Britain for at least six months of the year. At any minute of the day or night, during any conditions of tide and weather, they are out there doing something that can be explored to your advantage – as the holiday-maker and his rotten squid have so often proved.

A critical factor for the shore angler to consider is the clarity of the water. To some extent, this is tied in with how bright or dark the sky is, but I have never done well in thick, dirty water. Rarely have I caught bass from the chalk soup that gets churned up under the cliffs of Sussex. My best catches have been taken from cloudy – sometimes quite clear – water. This means fishing the surf when the wind is rising and the waves are building, or a day or two after a fierce blow. When the wind has been blowing a consistent Force 6 and drops away at sunset, that's one of my favourite times for fishing the rising tide.

A friend of mine, Nick Cranfield, always referred to 'the psychological moment', when he felt in his bones that now was the perfect moment to cast out the best crab from his bucket. He often caught a fish on it. We used to have a lot of fun fishing the rocks under Beachy Head and Seaford Head and shared some good catches together. Once I noticed a small hole under the rock he was standing on and pulled a perfect soft velvet swimming crab out from under his feet. We had had little luck gathering crabs that day, and this was the perfect 'psychological moment' bait. I tied it on, cast out, and caught a ten-pounder. From then on that particular outcrop was referred to as 'ten-pounder rock'.

I have yet to encounter a shore fishing mark where bass can be taken consistently throughout the tide. In most places there is a specific period – maybe as short as twenty minutes – when the chances of getting a take are at their highest. This is a problem for beginners to sort out, particularly nowadays. How does one decide whether the bass have moved on, aren't out there that day, or have been fished out completely?

One of my favourite 'psychological moments' is when the tide shows life at the start of the flood. This is often a reliable moment along low-lying reefs. Generally, you get a couple of hours of worthwhile fishing after the tide starts to push, but by half-tide

SHORE FISHING

SHORE FISHING

A fishing match on an Irish surf beach. Most bass specialists prefer to have the beach to themselves.

bites tend to fall off and you have to go to a different mark to fish the high water. Then you have to move to different marks for the ebb.

One of the attractions of bass fishing is working out what the fish are up to, and why. Years ago my friends and I used to catch a lot of fish from a short jetty 40yds (37m) down-tide of a long breakwater. From half-tide up, for two hours, there was every chance of getting fish, particularly if the swell was running with a big tide, but we never had takes around high water, and we could not work out why. I now think the bass were sheltering out of the tide.

Opposite: these three fine fish were caught the previous night, on frozen mackerel lobbed a few yards from the beach.

It runs swiftly along the beach and around the end of the breakwater. As the current eased, they left the shelter to go foraging along the steep shingle beach over the top of the tide.

Thunderingly big Atlantic surfs are uncomfortable for fish and rarely produce much. The bass avoid the swirling clouds of sharp sand, which probably irritate their gills. Big Irish surfs sometimes produce the odd very large bass, but the more gentle surfs are preferable. When bass are moving into shelter to get out of a big tide or bad weather, the first fish are often smaller ones, followed by larger ones. There may then be a lull of half an hour or more before the current and waves increase in strength and compel the nine to ten-pounders to seek shelter.

33

SHORE FISHING

Feeling for bites. I have caught dozens of bass from this little jetty.

by lobbing my bait out ten yards, just behind the first, small, breaking wave. All I caught was school bass, but each time I cast twenty yards or more, looking for bigger fish, they ignored my bait completely. Short casting is often essential when fishing from rocks (*see* chapter 3) and when fishing with plugs and other lures.

Long casting is rarely an advantage, unless you are trying to present a bait in a specific holding area offshore. A distant gully, sandbank, patch of rocks, or warm-water outfall may prove attractive to the bass. If these fish are big enough to be worth catching, the bait will normally be big and tough enough to fend for itself. A simple bait-clip can be used, rather than some of the more esoteric gadgets that are available from tackle shops. If the bait has a habit of flying off the hook, you are probably casting too far. Long casting occasionally brings benefits in light surf on very shallow beaches because there is insufficient wave action to focus the fish.

One of my favourite shore marks is a small bay, about 40yds (37m) wide, between a short jetty and a ramshackle wooden breakwater. My friends and I used to cast out to the sand or to a ridge of low rocks, but we eventually discovered that we caught many more fish by casting inshore from the jetty to a tiny shingle beach on the far side of the little bay. We noticed that, in moderately rough seas, the waves churn along the edge of the jetty, hit the rocks inshore, and then swill towards the little patch of shingle. It is this wave action, of course, that piles up the shingle there. Any food items that get washed out by the rough seas naturally end up there, too, and the bass know this. It is a 40yd (37m) cast, but the bait ends up about 5yds (4.5m) from the rocks behind the beach. Unfortunately it is too dangerous to fish directly from the rocks. Otherwise, we could use very light tackle.

Bass often go into very shallow water to collect a bait. They follow the scent trail for a long way and seem to be more intent on their goal than on the diminishing depth of water. It is not uncommon to see school bass attacking baitfish so close to the beach that they occasionally become stranded by a breaking wave and have to flap back into the water. Larger bass are quite content to forage in a foot or two of water, provided the sea is not too rough. On many occasions anglers have cast out much too far, way beyond the fish, and have caught nothing.

I have frequently caught bass consistently by casting a mere 25yds (23m). On one occasion the only way I could catch anything was

34

SHORE FISHING

Eastbourne Pier: bass shelter deep inside the structure, or lie in ambush around the piles.

BITES

Bass usually attack a bait with gusto, and sometimes they can be downright violent. I can recall three occasions when my bait was taken so aggressively that the line was snapped at the reel. The drag was not set particularly tight, but could not respond quickly enough to the shock. Nowadays I fish with a fairly light drag to avoid any repetition of this.

The classic bass bite from the shore is usually a sharp jolt, followed by a firm pull. Usually it is over within a second or two, and any failure to strike and set the hook allows the fish to escape, unless it has hooked itself. For this reason, most bass anglers hold their rod at all times. Some successful bassmen use a rod rest, but keep their eyes glued to the tip, ready to strike at the first sign of a take.

Rod rests are more trouble than they are worth when fishing shallow surf beaches because you have to keep an eye on them to ensure that they don't get dragged away by the undertow. Nor do they assist in the detection of the very gentle bites that bass sometimes give. They can give very little indication that they have taken the bait. The weight keeps slipping slightly, or you feel a gentle tremble on the line. There is neither a jolt nor a positive run, but sometimes when you strike these little bites you find that the fish has swallowed the bait right down. Perhaps it realizes

SHORE FISHING

that it has landed itself in deep trouble and is wondering how to get out of the predicament without giving itself away. If the rod were in a rest, it might easily do so.

I count myself extremely fortunate to have met and fished with some of Britain's top bassmen, but the man who made the greatest impact on my early years in the 1960s was a local angler, Eric Mesmer. Eric is now with the angels, but he taught me a huge amount about bass fishing, and was the first person to set me on the road to catching them consistently. I used to sit beside him on a little flint jetty beneath the cliffs, my legs dangling over the edge as I listened, entranced, to all the tales he had to tell of big fish landed, bigger fish lost, and the large shoals that used to swim around where he was fishing. Eric was a farmer and spoke in a soft voice, recounting anecdotes and fishing tales from years gone by. He must have been bass fishing for at least fifty years. He was absolutely adamant that bass don't often take a bait hard.

He used to fish with two whippy 7ft solid glass spinning rods and small fixed-spool reels. Before then, he had made rods out of old tank aerials. He would cast out and then lean the two rods against the rail along the edge of the jetty. He positioned them so that the tips were 2in (5cm) apart, so he could compare the two. Then he clove-hitched a bit of matchstick to his line so that it rested inside the tip ring. The idea was to eliminate stretch in the line between rod-tip and reel so that

Newhaven Harbour is a nursery area for bass fry and frequented by their parents under cover of darkness.

SHORE FISHING

Sometimes other species of fish do convincing impressions of bass bites. Eels, wrasse and flounders can set the adrenalin surging, but when they are around, a hefty strike is normally met by little resistance other than what you would expect when something small is wriggling on the end of the line. These bites, unfortunately, need to be taken seriously because at other times 'another poxy eel' turns out to be a rod-bending bass.

School bass can be frustrating. They pick up a bait that is intended for much larger specimens and dash away with it. The rod bends dramatically, but the strike connects with nothing. This may happen time and again as the schoolies grab the bait and make off with it, but as the bait is too large for them to swallow, they run off with it to distance themselves from other members of the shoal that may try to rob them of it. They hold the bait between their lips, and the strike just pulls it clear.

If this happens persistently, a very small bait can be mounted on a smaller hook and a tiny bass could be landed. However, tiny bass are not as desirable as larger specimens, so this trick can be self-defeating. A large bass may move into the swim and a small fragment of crab is unlikely to interest it, so it is much better to persevere with the schoolies and hope that a big fish is not far away. This does pay off sometimes, and the next pull on the line may be met by firm resistance and an angry splashing at the surface.

I prefer to hold my rod at all times and feel for bites. This allows me to detect the first signs of interest and to react positively to them. Generally, I hold the tip low and out of the wind, just above the waves and pointing down the line. I hold the rod in my right hand, with my thumb on the multiplier's spool, and a 2ft (60cm) loop of line in the left hand. Except in strong surf, I often fish with the reel out of gear, in case the fish requires more space – and line – before it accepts the

The pier at the mouth of a harbour or estuary is a traditional place for catching bass.

gentle bites showed up positively. You could call this an early (and somewhat primitive) version of the quiver-tip.

He obviously had a point because I often saw one of his rod-tips lean a couple of inches. A swift strike was followed by a plunging, jolting rod as a bass tried to make its escape. When you consider how many bass he caught in his lifetime, and how many he saw swimming around during those early years before the species became commercially exploited, it was a highly successful technique. However, it must also be said that the clove-hitching of a matchstick to the line can cause it to snap on the strike. This was what happened when I tried this trick, but Eric was a masterful practitioner of his craft.

37

SHORE FISHING

bait. The first sign of a take is generally a twitch on the rod-tip, which is generally seen before it is felt (if fishing in daylight). If the twitch is fairly gentle, it may be a suspicious fish, so I release the loop of line and wait for it to be pulled tight. The fish should have the bait inside its mouth by then, and I set the hook immediately the line tightens. If nothing happens soon, I tighten up again to make sure the fish is not swimming towards me.

Another reason for holding the rod is that you are in a better position to feel everything that happens to the bait. Small fish and crabs often nibble at it, and this attrition can leave a perfect, juicy offering looking like a soggy rag and lacking in bass appeal. You feel the sudden rattle as a pouting, wrasse or silver eel bites the back out of the peeler, or the gentle drawing as the surf picks up a crab that has fastened itself to the bait, or the little twitches when crabs are picking the bait apart (you can often see where the end of the trace has been crimped by their claws). Crab inactivity is often a very good indication of the presence of bass. When the crabs stop their pestering, I cast out my most tempting bait and have often had it taken straight away by a good

Keep the line tight during the closing stages of the fight, or the bass may shake its head and throw the hook.

I usually fish with the reel out of gear and holding a loop of line so bass can take the bait without feeling resistance.

bass. It seems as though the crabs scuttle for cover when bass are hunting the surf line.

Bite detection in surf can be tricky because of the line pinging off the water tables. If it gets bad, I sometimes put the rod-tip under water. The motion of the surf causes all sorts of phantom bites. The weight lifts suddenly, then drops again, or pressure on the line may suddenly increase, caused by a surge of surf or a succession of large waves. It pays to watch the surf and make sure that this interference is caused by large breakers. These movements lack the positiveness of a bass snatching at the bait. They take a little too long to happen and do not develop into anything.

Surf anglers can reduce the number of false bites by not casting so far and by ensuring that the line enters the surf at right angles, so that the water tables run up it rather than pushing it ahead of them. There are two ways of doing this. One is to cast out, then walk along the shore line until the line is entering the surf at the correct angle, even though it is being bowed by the wind. The second method is useful when you are fishing a specific area: walk up-tide or up-wind before casting out and the line should be fishing at the right angle when you resume your position. Bite detection is enhanced by reducing interference to the line. However, there is not much you can do when the water is littered with drifting weed.

No matter how the bass are biting, a very sharp hook is essential for converting takes into fish. A hook with a very sharp point has every chance of catching in a flap of skin inside the bass's bony mouth, so it is essential to check the point each time you reel in to inspect the bait. The easy way to do this is to stick it into the nail of your thumb. If it pricks in easily, it is sharp enough. If it skates over the top, a few strokes with the file are called for. Points can easily be blunted by rocks and stones that are found where bass feed.

STRIKING

Timing the strike is critical. At other times, you can do no more than hang on to the rod to prevent an enthusiastic fish from dragging it into the sea after hooking itself. Most times, bites have to be evaluated and the hook set at the right moment.

A lot depends on the fishing method that is in use, but I suppose that most of us fish on the bottom with either leger tackle or a running paternoster. As a general rule, it is sensible to set the hook the moment you feel that the bass has taken the bait properly into its mouth. This is easier said than done, of course, because so much depends on the direction in which the fish is swimming when it makes off with the bait.

If the bass moves slowly up-tide with the bait, swimming parallel to the beach, the angler feels no more than a deceptively gentle drawing on the line, and sometimes a slight twitching sensation. If the fish moves towards him, the line will fall slack. If it moves directly away, the result will be a firm pull. A fish that moves slowly down-tide with the bait may also cause a gentle drawing on the line. If the lead weight is felt bobbing and dragging over the sea-bed, the fish usually has a firm hold of the bait and should be struck. When fishing over sand, this dragging may not be felt. Instead, the line keeps slackening and a firm connection cannot be maintained to the weight. Sensitivity is often reduced by the tide and wind bowing the line, particularly when the wind is blowing with the tide along the beach. Bits of floating weed do not help either. Under these circumstances, the early taps and knockings can be drowned out, so anything fishy needs to be struck. On a few occasions, while fishing in borderline conditions, the first thing my friends and I have known about a bite was when the fish was seen thrashing on the surface, firmly hooked.

SHORE FISHING

Prawns are most effective when float fished tight to a structure, but a powerful rod is needed to control the fish.

mouth on the strike. One trick is to wind in slowly to keep in touch with the fish, and wait for it to turn away with the bait. Sometimes you have to keep winding and winding, as the bass swims closer and closer – exciting stuff.

When a bass gives a firm pull on the line, all that you usually have to do is pull back firmly with the rod to set the hook. I prefer to take a few rapid steps backwards at the same time to eliminate any slack or stretch in the line. This is often essential when dealing with a slack-line bite because there is one firm rule in angling that should always be observed: never strike with a slack line. The bass may only get pricked and may shed the hook before it feels the full pressure of the rod. However, when fishing the rocks, and especially at night, it can be downright dangerous to run backwards. It is much safer to point the rod at the fish, reel in like crazy until the line comes tight, and then set the hook – but don't do it so violently that the line snaps. A carbon-fibre rod can be rather unforgiving at short range on a tight, light line.

If in doubt, strike. Opportunities to set the hook into bass are sufficiently infrequent that it is best to try to convert every suspicious movement on the line into a hooked fish. It is very satisfying when a tentative strike is met by the thumping strain of a decent fish. In some places, slack-line bites are relatively straightforward because the bass has a firm enough grip on the bait to move the lead weight, so the response should be immediate. At other times, the bass has a light hold on the bait and it may be pulled out of the fish's

THE FIGHT

Bass usually fight best in clear water during daylight. When they are caught in clear, shallow water, they usually make long drag-screaming runs, which are magnificent. In fairly deep, clear water they have plenty of space in which to run and dive. Consequently, I envy all those anglers who have clear Atlantic water washing around the places where they fish. In Sussex, the inshore water is generally cloudy, especially during surfy conditions, and the bass rarely run much. Instead, they come to the surface as soon as they are hooked and thrash about violently, trying to throw the hook. A tight line is essential when they do this, keeping a good bend in the rod, or they may throw the hook.

SHORE FISHING

Sometimes they make an attempt to run and dive, but as they cannot see where they are going, these efforts are usually half-hearted. As a result, the fish arrives inshore with plenty of fight left in it. Naturally enough, this is disappointing, but any attempt to make the fish run will risk allowing it to throw the hook or snag the line around a rock.

In cloudy or clear water, bass fight the pressure of the rod by planing off to one side. This may take them into snags. With all due respect to the fish, it is sometimes best to haul them out of snaggy swims and forget about their sporting nature. Interestingly, most of the bass that are caught from a specific mark will fight in exactly the same manner.

In some places, the bass run inshore the moment they are hooked. Usually this requires the angler to wind in desperately until he regains contact with the fish. On a few occasions while fishing the surf at night, the bass have ended up closer to shore than the angler. Once I had a good laugh when a friend of mine, Larry Brumen, hooked a fish that left him with yards of slack line. He thought it had snapped and wound like crazy. Suddenly he picked up pressure. There was a tremendous thrashing behind his legs, and an eight-pounder surged back out to sea.

That certainly was a night to remember. It was one of those perfect tides, with a warm sou'westerly breeze, a steady surf, and lots of fish running. If we didn't get a take within ten minutes of casting, we started to become paranoid about the bait. I'll never forget the sight of Larry's rod bent double by a fish, the shadows of the breaking waves that were cast by a full moon riding above the cliffs behind him, and the bright, white clouds scudding across the sky. Nor will I ever forget my own rod being bounced around by the seven- and eight-pounders that took my bait. Nights like that are to be treasured.

Restraining a schoolie in a wet cloth for unhooking so as not to get jabbed by its sharp spines.

Some people have said that bass jump during the fight, but I have never seen one leap or leave the water in any other way while fighting – other than a schoolie being unceremoniously bundled ashore for release. The only time I have seen a bass do anything like this was when a friend of mine struck a fish in 18ins (45cm) of gin-clear water after it had dropped the bait. The bass shot out of the water like a missile. I have had freshwater eels do the same, also in very shallow water.

41

SHORE FISHING

LANDING

Before starting to fish, you need a clear idea of where the bass are to be beached or landed. Even though you may only be expecting schoolies, large bass are nomadic buccaneers so you should never rule out the possibility of hooking a fourteen-pounder – or bigger. To avoid heartbreak, proper landing gear is required, be it a landing net or a drop net. Bass are much too noble to be gaffed, but if you have to use such a primitive tool, nick the fish under the chin. This permits it to be returned alive, if so desired. Should you be faced by a twenty-five-pounder that has just thrown the hook and is lying gasping at the surface, put the gaff beyond the fish, lower it under its own weight, then pull it home into the cheek. Slashing at fish with gaffs is a good way of tangling the line, knocking the hook free, and generally losing them.

The way to use a drop net is to lower it where the waves cause least disturbance. Draw the fish over the net, then lift in one smooth operation. I must confess that I have rarely fished in places where a drop-net would be required. There is usually somewhere that a landing net can be used – keeping an eye out for dangerous waves as you do so, of course.

Some anglers stab at fish with landing nets, but that is completely wrong. The fish knows that it is in serious trouble and is trying

A fine catch of six-pounders, all taken within twenty yards of the edge of a reef.

SHORE FISHING

A landing net is sometimes handy but is usually an encumbrance for the beach fisherman.

SHORE FISHING

to work out why. It should be frightened as little as possible, or it may panic, snap the line and escape. With the minimum of fuss and shouting, the net is sunk below the level of the fish. The fish is then drawn closer to the surface, followed by the net, and is enmeshed before it realizes what has happened. If the tide is running and the fish is hanging in the current, it helps to have an assistant. To give the man with the net sufficient space, walk a few paces uptide, bring the fish to the surface, then gently ease off the pressure so that it drifts, tail first, into the landing net. Don't give it slack line, or it may throw the hook, and never try to lift or drag it by handling the line. For some reason, anything under a 20lb line usually snaps, and you're left cursing your foolishness as a chunky fish raises a fin and waves goodbye.

Even when fishing from a jetty, it is often easiest to walk the fish to the beach or some other convenient landing site. The first thing, however, is to play it out so that it has little fight left. Towards the closing stages of the fight, provided that the fish is clear of obstacles and snags, it should be allowed to have its head and tire itself out in preparation for landing. A bass of any size should always be allowed to have its say, no matter how desperate you are to get a look at it.

Most of the time it is simply a case of drawing the fish into the shallows, then taking hold of a gill-cover and sliding it up the sand or shingle, or into a rock pool, out of reach of the water. Keep the fingers clear of the gills and the gill rakers, which are sharp. Do not drag it far if you wish to return it to the water, lest you damage its protective layer of mucus. If a fish is to be kept, it should be dispatched immediately, while it is still in shock after its sudden encounter with fresh air. It is undignified – for both angler and fish – for bass to be left flapping around.

Bass are normally easy to unhook because large hooks are used to catch them and they have an enormous mouth that allows plenty of room for manoeuvre. Even a 6/0 looks lost inside the mouth of a decent fish. Fish that are to be returned should be wrapped in a soaking wet towel, and the hook removed. A pair of forceps or long-nosed pliers may be useful for stubborn hooks. If the fish has the bait inside its stomach, there is a trick for getting it out. Find the butt end of an old fishing rod and cut a rod 18in (45cm) long. Plug each end with a piece of cork and cut a deep notch across the thick end to take the trace. Carefully poke the thin end into the fish's stomach, hold the trace in the notch, and twist the rod so the trace winds around it and pulls the hook out backwards.

TACKLE AND CLOTHING

When I started bass fishing, the available tackle was appalling. Many anglers still used Burma poles, or greenheart rods and starback centrepin reels. Most nylon line was unreliable, at best. Knots cracked apart, and sometimes it snapped like cotton. Much of my angling career has been spent, file in hand, making things which are nowadays widely available as standard items from a tackle shop. Not that this really applies to my bass fishing, because I have always travelled as light as possible. A simple rod, reel, fresh line, a couple of swivels, a light bomb, a decent hook, and strong knots can be relied on to catch more bass than any other type of tackle.

Rods

Most shore fishing for bass is undertaken with a standard 11ft rod, casting 2–3oz (55–85g) weights, together with a light multiplier or fixed-spool reel, depending on your preference. Most tackle dealers carry a range of light rods that are more than equal to the task and a wide range of beautifully designed reels.

SHORE FISHING

One from the family album: I was sixteen and the clear, calm sea was swarming with bass, but they did not want my lugworm.

Quite a few 11ft carbon-fibre bass rods are available today, and they are light years ahead of the tackle that I was compelled to use when I first started out. It would be pointless for me to mention specific models when so many good rods are available. Besides, the tackle itself is not nearly so important as your ability to use it in the right manner, in the right place and at the right time.

Nevertheless, I think that a bass rod should have a fast action and a fine tip. It balances well in the hand, enabling the angler to detect bites but limits the bass's ability to detect the angler. I once fished a night tide with a light, but powerful, cod rod because I had left my proper bass rod on my boat and could not be bothered to go and fetch it. Quite a few bass were milling around the estuary mouth, waiting to run up-river, and I got several offers, but the rod tip was so stiff that the fish were feeling it and dropping the bait before I could strike. I eventually landed a nine-pounder, but I would have caught more if I had taken a proper bass rod with me.

A bass rod looks like a simple thing but it takes years to know how to handle it. The best rods that I have ever used are built on blanks made by Michael McManus at Conoflex and by Terry Carroll at Zziplex. I am fortunate that both of these gentlemen are old friends, and I have been able to test some excellent prototypes. Come to think of it, most of my rods are prototypes. It must be time I bought a proper bass rod.

The trouble is that many modern rods have a rigid butt and a very fast tip, which is all very fine for casting to the horizon, but is self-defeating with bass fishing because the fish are usually close to the edge. I would hazard a guess that most bass from the shore have been caught with fairly through-action rods. They need to be moderately fast, but I like to see a lot of rod bending when hustling a big fish, and it is best if I can feel the action under my hand on the butt. What I do not like is the sensation of fishing with a pole with a whisker at the end, which is the current interpretation of the word 'fast'.

A rod with a fast action has a lot of backbone for casting out large baits and controlling hooked fish. Bass are often caught from extremely graunchy swims, and the rod needs to be powerful enough to set the hook into the bony mouth and bully the fish away from the snags. Sometimes an 11ft carp rod is quite adequate, especially in gentle surfs, calm seas and inside estuaries. Rods like this, with about a 2lb test curve, also double as spinning rods.

It is always interesting to check a rod at home by tying the line to a tree and seeing

45

SHORE FISHING

A rod rest is more trouble than it is worth for surf fishing.

how the reel and drag perform as the rod bends. (Never strike at a tree, or the rod may snap. Even bass do have some give!) This does help to evaluate the action and see if the rings are in the right place. I have painted the top 18in (45cm) of my bass rods with white gloss paint so that the bites may be seen before they are felt, particularly when the rod is at rest when I'm boat fishing.

Reels

Bass do not require a huge amount of line, so a bulky reel is not necessary. I prefer to use multipliers for everything other than lure fishing, float fishing or free-lining. The Ambassadeur 6500C is my favourite for shore fishing, but for big fish in deep water, I prefer the Ambassadeur 7000.

Tackle needs to be properly maintained for fighting lunker bass.

SHORE FISHING

There are lots of very good makes and models of reels, particularly fixed spool reels. They should have a smooth, positive drag and be solidly constructed and salt-water proof. All reels need to be maintained in perfect order for when that ten-pounder comes looking for you.

I am not a fan of washing my reels after use, unless one has been dunked in the sea. Alloy sideplates can be protected on the inside with a light smear of waterproof grease. Otherwise, the best attention mine get is a wipe with kitchen paper. Once or twice a year they are stripped to their nuts and bolts, cleaned, lubricated, reassembled, and filled with a new line. Do not leave a wet reel to rot in a damp case in a damp corner or it will let you down at a critical moment.

Lines

As a general rule, 10–16lb line is best for open beaches and surf fishing, and 25–30lb amid the snags. Rocks, concrete, flints and rusting ironwork are no respecters of fine tackle, and it is not sporting to use line that is too light to contend with snaggy swims. I hate it every time a fish snaps me off against a flint or a jagged lump of metal because it leaves the hook in the fish. This is why I never use treble hooks when fishing with bait. Bass often gulp down their food. If one were lost, gut hooked with a treble, it might be unable to feed. I much prefer a single hook.

Line needs to be strong, with sound knots and neat traces. The last few yards should always be checked when reeling in, feeling every inch for nicks and abrasions. Big bass are not going to play gentle just because the line is rotten.

Lighter line, about 10lb, is best for float fishing and spinning. Ten pound line is also fun in moderate surf, although a 25lb shock leader may be required. For maximum strength, I form a Bimini loop in the main line and tie the leader to this with a nail knot. Other types of leader knot regularly fail. They all collect weed while reeling in. Light line is handy for lead links which are intended to snap if they get caught in a snag – the rotten bottom. I like them really rotten when casting a short distance; 6lb is ideal.

Superbraid lines, like Dyneema, and other molecularly aligned polypropylene lines are supremely thin, have insignificant stretch, and resist abrasion better than nylon. Every crab can be felt looting the bait a hundred yards away, but they are a mixed blessing. A fishing line is a vehicle for a two-way experience. What you feel, the fish feels, so the bass are much more able to detect the rod-tip when they pick up the bait, or the jolt as the multiplier spool starts spinning to the take, and perhaps even light pressure from your thumb. From a boat, the jolts from bass taking a bait down-tide can easily cause a well-loaded spool to over-run, so it is unwise to take the thumb off the spool. The problem is that superbraids are too fierce. Years ago my hand was sliced practically to the bone when I got a violent take from a six-pounder, which dragged a tight finely braided line across my finger. All I was doing was holding the regulation loop of line while feeling for the first sign of interest.

Elasticity is a useful cushion between the bass and the angler at all stages of catching and landing. I am certain that some of the ten- to twelve-pounders my friends and I have caught from wrecks would have straightened the hook and escaped if we had used superbraid. The thumping, shoulder-jolting fight of a big bass in deep water would probably tear the hookhold considerably. Hook points that are good at cutting their way into a fish can also cut their way back out again.

This point of contact is precious. It may be very precarious, but a hookhold at the tip of the lip has often proved strong enough to withstand the ensuing struggle. Sound nylon, with

SHORE FISHING

Floats should be big enough to support a large bait and remain visible in choppy water.

its extra give, can endure no end of abrasion and still allow the angler to pile on pressure when the fight turns into a tug of war. Like a bungee, the strain increases on the knots and the hookhold gradually. Some carbon-fibre rods are unforgiving and under some circumstances smash takes would be precisely that.

One compromise is to use a long nylon header. This reduces the chances of abrasion at the business end and avoids the need to tie Bimini loops more than once a month. A leader also absorbs any thrashing and banging at that critical moment when a fish is being prepared for landing.

None the less, Dyneema is soft, extremely thin for its strength, and has good abrasion resistance. Maybe it will turn out to be better for traces than for main lines, or for making hair rigs. A hair rig is useful to attach a large bait to a small hook. The bait is tied onto the hair, which is attached to the hook.

Never throw waste line – or any plastic – into the sea. Nylon line is deadly to sea-birds and wildlife, even when tangled up in a ball. I often see gannets that have seen something glittering under the water and have accurately speared a ball of nylon line. Unless they can get rid of it they are destined to starve.

Hooks

Bass hooks should always be razor-pointed. I generally use only one pattern, the Mustad 79515, and its older brother, the 79510 – the shibboleth of bass anglers throughout Britain. The smaller sizes are useful for smaller baits, but I have caught a lot of fish on the 4/0 size. A 6/0 79515 is more convenient for big baits, and some bassmen bend the point out slightly to increase its bite. I have never had any of these hooks snap on me and I have frequently been amazed at how much stick they will take from big fish – and from snags. They have a slim profile that sits wickedly in a bait.

I like hooks with small barbs and fairly short points for easy penetration, and even then I may take a small triangular file to them and make them sweeter – or a nailfile covered with diamond dust, which is less likely to rust. A smear of grease keeps files from being blunted by rust.

The 79510 has a strong, forged bend, unlike the feeble Aberdeen hook which is too springy for my liking and may release a fish when pulled to the limit. I test a few of each batch of hooks I buy to see if they are strong enough. Poke some 50lb line through the eye, tie the ends together, put the hook around a

SHORE FISHING

nail, and pull the other end of the loop with a spring balance. If it lets you bounce it up to 20lb a few times, it – and its mates – should be strong enough. Some hooks ping apart, so wear glasses or goggles to protect your eyes.

Always buy lots of hooks, by the box of fifty or a hundred if possible. Plenty of them get snagged up and lost, and if you are not catching many bass, you are probably not losing enough hooks.

Lead Weights

If you make leads, make plenty to see you through a few seasons. It is by far the best way. Wear safety goggles. Before I go fishing, I clear out the wire eye and attach a clip to save time and trouble later on. Clips are essential to preserve knots when reeling in over shingle beaches and save on abrasion on surf beaches.

Surf pyramids of 2–3oz (57–85g) with long wire tails are useful on sandy storm beaches, or lightly wired breakout leads. Where there is little tide-run along a beach, small bombs of 1½–2oz (43–57g) are adequate. In calm conditions, in sheltered corners, it is often no trouble to fish with ¾oz (21g), sometimes no lead at all. As a general rule, the less lead the better, provided that you can fish properly.

Occasionally 5–6oz (142–170g) of lead (and a rod to match) may be required for long casting or to anchor the bait down in a strong tide-run, but I have found that wherever the tide was strong enough to sweep my bait ahead of it, few bass would be found. Where the current is strong, the fish wait in ambush, and that normally turns out to be a quiet corner or a deeper hole where the tide runs past overhead.

Terminal Tackle

I use the same simple rig for nearly all my bass fishing, and that is two small black swivels with a lead link coming off one and the hook trace off the other. The lead link swivel is allowed to run along the line, and the hook swivel is tied to the end. The swivels should not be so small that the one for the lead link jams on the knot of the other. Some people use split rings, but I do not like them. Beads are unnecessary. This set-up allows the bass to take line without feeling the weight and enables me to detect the bite before the fish realizes I am there. When used with a 30in (76cm) lead link and an 8in (20cm) trace, it is a running paternoster. When the trace is lengthened and the lead link shortened, it becomes a running leger.

The calmer the conditions are, the longer the trace – up to 6ft (1.8m), if necessary – and it is practical to cast it out there. Long traces are prone to tangle in surf and rough seas, particularly when big baits are in use, and they often come back like knitting. It pays to tie up traces in advance so that if a set of tackle is lost to a snag, a fresh bait can be cast out within a few moments. This allows you to take advantage of those brief periods when the bass are in front of you, before they move on.

Ancillary Items

Some other bits of tackle are useful. A small torch, worn on a thong around the neck, is useful for baiting up at night, and so is a Petzel headlight. Spare bulbs should always be carried and a spare set of batteries.

Film canisters (35mm), made of clear plastic, are excellent for storing small items of tackle and keeping them away from salt and dirt. It is easy to see what is inside them. Film processors should be able to give you some if you ask them nicely.

As for weighing scales, I have a tubular brass spring balance, made by the House of Hardy, which weighs up to 22lb (10kg). It is completely accurate. It may not be the most precise, but I have scant interest in half ounces

SHORE FISHING

and drams. If a 9lb bass has just eaten a 1lb pouting, is it then a ten-pounder? Avon scales, like those used by freshwater specimen hunters, are much too bulky. My only interest in the weight of a fish is to find out if it has edged over that magic 10lb mark. Bass fishing is bass fishing, and provided that every opportunity is taken to allow the fish to show its fighting verve, the size does not really matter. I love going out and catching schoolies on fly tackle or spinning for them in a tide-race.

That vicious strike is equally exciting in skinny water when catching small fish on light tackle, as it is out deep when five- to ten-pounders are the quarry. I have to say that when a double-figure fish strikes in deep water, all you can do is hang on. The take is like somebody tying a 10lb (4.5kg) weight to your line, then dropping it. Every year I can't resist educating the schoolies when I find them ganging up on a calm evening, chasing the baitfish. They are such suckers for the lure and hit it so fiercely that I have spent many happy hours shaking them free and watching them dart away.

The fact that the bass record has hovered just under 20lbs for so long has made the catching of an ten-pounder a highly significant event. Days like this are relived many times, but the mathematics are also perfectly balanced. No matter what species of fish is considered, the specimen weight is always half of the record. A good, but modest, fish weighs half that, and one to be returned at a minimum sporting size, half that: 20–10–5–2½lb. Sport-fishing weights for bass will be a long time in going metric because they already have their own metric logic.

Most anglers nick the weighing hook under the fish's chin, but that is not kind if the fish is to be put back alive. It is better to use a weighing sling.

Bait rags are essential for drying your hands after rinsing them in the sea. Ask your local pub (especially if it serves draught Bass) to donate a few towelling beer mats. They are small, highly absorbent and conveniently shaped. They could have been designed to keep anglers' fingers clean.

For a priest, I carry the 14in glass-fibre butt spigot of a tournament casting rod on my boat to rap bass hard across the skull, behind the eyes. From the shore, I leave long, slim flints in rock pools close by my favourite marks, or long bolts that may have held sea defences or a ship together. You often find things like this while crabbing (even wartime bombs and mines, so beware), so it is no trouble to obtain a suitable weapon and plonk it in a pool near where the fish are caught.

Beaches can get very cold at night or when a sea fog rolls in by day, so a spare bodywarmer may be advisable. Many quilted designs are light and unobtrusive. For colder conditions, I favour a jacket with a lining of nylon fur.

Waders (both breast-high for surf, and thigh-high for general use) are essential, and so are reliable waterproofs – both jacket and overtrousers. I prefer a jacket with large pockets because I usually carry my tackle in them. A small haversack can be useful for sandwiches and a drink, or a bum-bag. A peaked hat and Polaroid sunglasses protect the face in blindingly bright weather and enable cruising fish to be spotted. If you plan to go away surf fishing for a few days, take a hair dryer fitted with a long hose to dry out your waders. Clammy boots rapidly lead to cold feet.

It is very important to keep a fishing diary. It is as vital as rod and reel. It enables the forthcoming season to be planned in advance. By referring to the tide chart, you will not overlook opportunities to catch bass. Afterwards, a full record needs to be written down, detailing place, method, bait, tide, weather, time, and everything else you saw or heard that day. Big desk diaries are often sold cheaply in the New Year. Some details may seem insignificant at the time, but as the seasons roll by, patterns emerge that assist you to catch more bass.

3 Where to Find Bass Inshore

Where to find feeding bass is the sixty-four-thousand dollar question. Fortunately many of the hot-spots are well known, yet it seems to be the fate of bass anglers to have to rediscover some of the old hot-spots and learn anew how to fish them. Bass have been caught from many secret, treasured corners around the British Isles and some of the old bassmen have moved on and taken their secrets with them.

This is only as it should be because most bass anglers prefer the beach to themselves and their chosen companion. The sight of another angler within a mile is considered to be a crowd. Even today, there are times and tides when no solitary figure can be seen standing in the surf, even in perfect conditions when the fish are running. That, of course, is a good thing: the last thing we want in bass fishing is time-share, a disease that has recently struck salmon fishing.

Big bass sometimes give very gentle bites, even in strong surf.

WHERE TO FIND BASS INSHORE

I have often been surprised at how small the area is where bass are prepared to accept a bait. Cast outside this zone, and bites become scarce. This is not universal, but you should always try to find the precise swim that interests the fish, rather than hope they are desperate for the bait.

I am now going to try to generalize every shore fishing situation around Britain, with advice on how to tackle it. This may seem a foolhardy thing to do, but bass are sufficiently regular in their habits to permit me a stab at it.

Bass feed in two distinct ways. They either move around searching for prey or they hang around a specific area waiting for the tide to carry prey to them. On occasions, large shoals of bass can be seen milling around in the surf, although few may be keen to take conventional baits. I have never heard of anglers making big catches when large numbers of bass can be seen. It could be that they have been trapped inshore by tope, porpoises or sharks working behind the surf line. Although this is hard to confirm, some of the old-time bass anglers told me about such happenings.

It seems to be the instinct of bass to stay out of clear, shallow water by day, particularly over open sand. No doubt sharks and porpoises have drummed this into them over the last few million years. They are happy to move into clear shallow water where disturbance is slight, especially at night or where they can make a quick getaway into rocks and gullies. If the water is stirred up and moderately cloudy, the fish feel much more confident. The important thing is the shallowness of the water. When a shoal of bass is disturbed, the first thing it does is dive towards the sea-bed. If the water is too shallow for this mode of escape, they feel nervous, unless a refuge can be found close by.

Every bass angler should have the word 'structure' indelibly inscribed onto his mind. Bass are frequently found close to structures because they offer security both to them and to their prey. The sort of structure that they like is fairly easy to identify. It contains holes, caves and gullies where the fish can hole up when not feeding. There are several variations on this theme: piles of large boulders, reefs with deep gullies, harbour walls and sea defences made of concrete blocks, old wrecks, piers that stand on a mass of girders, harbour installations and the like. The larger the structure, the more bass are likely to live around it. The main proviso is that their places of shelter be covered for most, or all, of the tide. Bass are less likely to be found where they are driven out by the ebbing tide. This should not be confused with catching them as they drop back along the shore with the ebb or return to the mouth of an estuary.

Bass seem to roam around more by night than they do by day and they can be ambushed when they come out to feed at dusk. This usually means tossing a bait into their likely route, possibly assisted by groundbait to bring the fish around. Another good time to catch them is shortly after dawn when they are moving back after their night's hunting.

I have never done particularly well by fishing featureless open beaches, except in a good surf. I much prefer to fish close to a structure, particularly if it is something like a headland at the end of the beach. I have caught more fish from the surf where the sand gives way to rock than I have by fishing from the middle of a featureless beach. The bass are much more likely to be persuaded towards the middle if it has rough, crabby ground or a river draining over it. Bass cannot resist exploring any outflow of fresh water, no matter how small, unless it is thick and peat-stained.

Every beach has an up-tide end and a down-tide end, i.e. the end towards which the current flows. On some beaches, bass are caught more frequently from the down-tide end than from anywhere else, and I assume

WHERE TO FIND BASS INSHORE

that this is where the tide washes the food. This is not a hard-and-fast rule because I have done very well at the up-tide end of some open beaches, but usually ones that are bordered by reefs. If the beach is under ¼ mile (0.4km) wide, there is a good chance of catching bass anywhere along it. Many anglers have a secret little beach and know precisely when the bass visit it. Information like this has often been won the hard way, which makes success taste sweeter.

Bass shoals may run the surf at any time, but are usually found there on the rising tide. They move through in waves, and one is treated to a series of pulls, offers and a fish or two before they move on and the sea suddenly seems lifeless. The best time is often when the rising tide coincides with nightfall, particularly when spring tides are building. However, it would be impossible for me to list when to fish specific areas. This knowledge has to be gleaned the hard way or worked out from what other anglers have – or have not – caught.

Bass can be caught from steep shingle beaches by day or by night. The depth of water gives them confidence, but even so they are more often found close in at night. The deeper the water, the less dependent you need to be on the surf for success. I prefer to fish those beaches when a sea is running but not when large rollers are roaring up the shingle. The trouble is that these steep beaches occasionally yield double-figure bass under such conditions.

I have caught a lot of bass on fillets of mackerel in August in calm, clear seas, and also in October on squid when the water has become cloudy after storms. Most steep beaches give way to sand, and sometimes a gully runs along the beach where the sand meets the shingle. This is the best place for the bait, which should be large and appetizing. If the beach is backed by a sea wall, bass are sometimes found patrolling along it at high tide. Similar fishing can be found in several other areas. Headlands and promontories attract bass and sometimes concentrate them close to shore.

Chest-high waders and efficient waterproofs are essential for a rough day in the surf.

WHERE TO FIND BASS INSHORE

SURF FISHING

I have been fortunate to fish many of the great clear water Atlantic storm beaches in Wales, Cornwall, and Kerry – from Cefn Sidan to Stradbally. The pristine sand and powerful rollers make them wonderful places to fish. Sometimes the waves look dauntingly large, but they usually produce fish if tackled in the right way. Surf fishing is such a physical experience that most anglers stand among the water tables, but the right clothing is necessary for this. Modern neoprene chest-high waders are lightweight and warm, but they need to be worn with a pair of proper brogues that keep out the sand. They can be hot and are not easy to walk in, so it is best to carry them to a distant beach and put them on there. Once I acquired a pair of thin, latex chest-high waders. The first time I wore them, they started to fall apart at the crotch as I walked down to the surf. They leaked incessantly thereafter.

Thigh-waders are acceptable, but they need to be worn with overtrousers. The bib-and-brace design is best, but you need to make sure that they do not have gussets to provide access to your trouser pockets. The ankles should be wrapped around the boots and kept tight with water-proof tape, thick rubber bands or slices of inner tube to keep the water out. A water-proof jacket and a hood are essential, especially in an Irish downpour. A belt around the waist keeps out slapping waves.

A bum-bag on the belt, or a surf-bag is handy for surf fishing and other types of fishing when mobility is required. The belt makes a useful rod holder when both hands are needed for rebaiting. I prefer to keep bait and tackle in my pockets. The bait needs to be in a container or your pocket will soon start stinking. Cut the top off a plastic bottle and use

An Atlantic storm beach is the most beautiful and physical place to catch bass.

WHERE TO FIND BASS INSHORE

that for fresh worms, squid, crab or shellfish.

Sand can be a problem. It easily gets into the reel or rod ferrules, so never lay down the rod. A small paintbrush is useful for flicking away sand. If the reel accidentally gets jammed with the stuff, rinse it in the surf, but wash in fresh water later.

Most surf fishermen use a standard paternoster rig to cast into the wind and a single short trace so that it does not get balled up by the suds. In more temperate sea conditions, it is fun to wander along the beach and explore it with a rolling leger. This is impossible in a big surf as it throws the tackle straight back onto the beach.

Long casting is unnecessary because the fish may be very close at times. Remember that the water tables are pushing food ahead of them, and the backwash is concentrating the shrimps, small flatfish, squid and crabs in a narrow band some 30–80yds (27–73m) out – perhaps even closer. Lugworm, razor-fish, clam, squid, and all the usual baits catch bass in the surf. Mackerel strip and sandeels sometimes catch sea trout, and big thick-lipped mullet are caught from the more sheltered beaches. Peeler crab is very good for fat flounders. In some places, shoals of sprats come into the surf line, and they make a very good bait because they are so highly visible.

Surf bass normally fight by kiting away from the pressure of the rod and make reasonable runs. The dangerous time comes when trying to coax them through the undertow; which they use to their advantage. Never try to drag a big bass through the undertow; that invariably leads to disaster. They need to be treated carefully when the water is taking them back out to sea. Let them go, and bring them in with the next wave, gradually working them closer to shore. Another trick is to walk backwards along the beach, so that the side of the fish is exposed to the surf. This helps to roll it ashore, but it works better on steep beaches.

Any fish that can hold its own where the environment is churned to froth is not stupid. Even in a riotous, rolling surf bass are often quick to feel resistance, and they blow out the bait instantly. There is a slight draw, a quick knock, then nothing, and the fish continues on its way.

Bass sometimes roam over the white-water beaches when the sea is calm, but they are not concentrated into a specific area by the surf and backwash, and may be anywhere from the edge out to deeper water. A flat, surfless surf beach in bright sunny weather is not ideal for fishing, but there is always a better chance of finding fish after dark.

Drifting weed is the surf angler's nightmare, especially after a blow, but provided the filaments are not creating a minestrone and are confined to odd shreds, piles of kelp, and the occasional strand of wrack and oarweed, the bass are not bothered. If it is bad for you, it is worse for the bass, and they stay out of it. When fishing ceases to be fun, it is time to head for the pub. Weed is infuriating stuff at times but the bass love where it grows, so we have to endure these things – and how better than with a pint in hand? On some beaches, weed can be there on one tide and gone the next, or it may drift away as the tide increases in strength.

BEACHES

A very modern problem for anglers who fish some remote beaches is having their car stolen, vandalized, or set on fire while they are away fishing. In some cases this may be done by anti-hunting and fishing terrorists, but usually it is simple vandalism. Be warned.

Another problem is mislaying tackle. If you dump your kit on the beach or the rocks while bait collecting, make sure the rod sticks up and the tackle is in a recognizable area. It is amazing how much time can be wasted looking for tackle in the growing dusk. Put it

WHERE TO FIND BASS INSHORE

where you cannot fail to find it. Some anglers have spent ages searching and have missed the best part of the tide.

The ebb and flow of the tide are more important inshore than offshore, where all that happens is that the current changes direction and the sea gets a bit deeper or shallower. Inshore, and when beach fishing, the influence of the tide is much more pronounced. Currents flow along the beach, and the foreshore is stripped bare. This affects the behaviour of the bass, so always look at your watch after landing a fish – or missing a take. Their habits are so regular that they are usually caught at exactly the same state of tide. This regular behaviour is probably caused by the suitability of the tide for feeding at that stage. The beach fisherman has to find the bass then fish for them as best he may. It is always easiest to persuade a wild quarry species to do something that it wants to do anyway, so anglers need to ensure that their methods comply with the fish's intentions. It is important to put in the hours, watch the sea and learn from it all. Perseverance catches fish.

The first two hours of the flood tide are often the most productive because this is when the crabs, blennies and other small creatures of the inter-tidal zone vacate their low-water hiding places and start marching back up the beach to see what edible things they can find. The low tide compels them to congregate together, but as the water covers the beach, they disperse and the bass have less chance of catching them. The last of the ebb and the low tide period sometimes produce fish, but they usually turn up the moment the flood tide starts moving. They make the most of the scuttling hordes, hoping to find them tumbled by the waves. As the prey might be swirled away and lost, bass usually grab the bait firmly, with that classic, abrupt pull. It can be very abrupt at times if the hook is not set quickly.

When the weed gets this bad, it's time to retire for a pint of Guinness.

A peeler crab makes a good bait anywhere. The most usual bite a bass gives on a peeler is a tap or two, then a firm pull. Occasionally it hooks itself, but that should never be relied on. The first tap is the bass having a go at the crab and testing how much opposition it is likely to encounter. When it discovers that your carefully prepared peeler is a tatty meal that has no intention of fighting back, it gulps it down, and goes looking for the next one. That is when you get that classic pull. This is the moment to drag the hook into the fish. Give it a moment longer, and it will drop the bait, and the strike will come up against empty water. It is a hollow feeling. I can still vividly remember a sparkling June morning when a lively, glittering surf was running and crabs were peeling everywhere, but I could not hook a single fish.

It was perfect, until a stranger turned up. Another angler was on my beach, and he was collecting 'my' crabs. He even went to fish 'my' surf beach. That was years ago, but my defence is that it is a very small beach, and the taking area only 20–40yds (18–37m) wide. The upshot was that I was so uptight about this that I could not time my strike right. I had loads of takes, but I did not set the hook into a single fish. An hour or so later it was all over, and the other angler left the beach with two ten-pounders, an eight and a six. You can see why the day is indelibly etched on my mind.

Another time, the failure was much more funny. Three of us were fishing from a little jetty, and because it wasn't quite time for the bass to arrive, our rods were leaning against the rail. Suddenly a bass bounced my friend's rod and departed. As I went to pick up my rod, the tip bounced to another bite, then there was nothing. 'I had better hold my rod', said my other friend. As he went to do so, the tip was dragged hard over. Then nothing. We got three bites in little more than a minute, but none for the rest of the evening.

Steep Beaches

The steeper the beach, the closer the fish are likely to be and the shorter the cast unless some structure farther out attracts them. Many anglers fish the gully at the bottom of the shingle bank, but the bass are often much closer than that, particularly at night. Very large bass are found inshore after rough weather in the spring but more usually from September through to Christmas. Several are caught each season on shellfish, lug, crab, squid and fish. They prefer a big bait nailed hard down on the bottom with a short trace.

It is often more productive to fish in the lee of groynes, jetties and ledges in rough conditions. Bass shelter at the edge of the tide, where it swirls around the end of the jetty. Another place to try is the windward side of a solid pier, casting out a fair way. The wind pushes the waves along the shore line towards the pier and along the pier towards the beach. Where they meet, a fierce undertow is formed, and it drifts out to sea at an angle of 45 degrees. It is not easy to fish under these conditions, but the bass are usually still there when the wind drops. This trick is also good for reservoir trout fishing, when a current of clear water is being pushed along the dam wall and dirty water is coming along the shore line. It is often possible to find big trout in the undertow.

Calm Conditions

I am fairly certain that bass prefer to hunt in clear water if they have a choice. They are often found in very shallow, skinny water when they can see what they are doing. Around headlands, dirty water concentrates hunting bass into the lanes of clear water, and sometimes these persist close to shore when the sea-bed farther out is being ripped apart by spring tides. It is always worth standing on the clifftops and studying the shore line through binoculars at different states of the tide. I am fortunate to live only half a mile from the edge of the cliff, and it is a good place for walking the dogs.

You can see how the water is discoloured offshore by sand that has been kicked up by fierce spring tides, and the streaks of silt along the shore line. You can see where clear water persists inshore and also where surf breaks over reefs and where the crabbers have set their pots. The flow of the tides and the changing winds cause the water to vary in cloudiness, although this is very much influenced by where you are fishing. Some coastal waters are a lot grubbier than others.

WHERE TO FIND BASS INSHORE

In calm weather, when the water is clear, bass hunt shallow sandy beaches between dawn and sunrise. My guess is that their prey has less room to escape in shallow water. With their scorching turn of speed, the bass have little trouble catching anything that flushes ahead of them.

Even in hot, bright conditions, it is sometimes possible to see bass cruising along close to the shore, often right in the margin. This usually happens along fairly steep beaches and close to ledges. It is wonderful to see the tips of bass tails as they cruise around a weedbed. When they are just a few feet away, they give the appearance of large, white-fringed, grey torpedoes. I have been told that these fish are patrolling, but the ones I see never seem to come back. Perhaps they have followed the tide.

In calm, clear conditions, when they have plenty of time to inspect the bait warily and tweak it gently, bass sometimes need to be fished for with all the craft of a carp fisherman, but without the bite alarms and buzzers. The calmer the sea, the more time you have to allow a bass to take the bait. Several minutes may pass before the fish accepts your offering. Very big fish often give the most gentle of takes. In quiet water, the tiniest drawing on the line may be felt, then a small tap before it slackens again. Hopefully this fish has not dropped the bait.

Unless the fish are rampaging among baitfish, bait presentation needs to be perfect or the bass may become suspicious. It is best to let a taking fish make off with the bait and deal with it before reeling up tight and setting the hook. If you fail to hook the fish and it feels the point, it is unlikely to come back to the same bait a second time, although it might take your friend's bait.

I strongly suspect that when a fish escapes, it often takes the rest of the shoal with it. Sometimes a fish is lost when the line snaps,

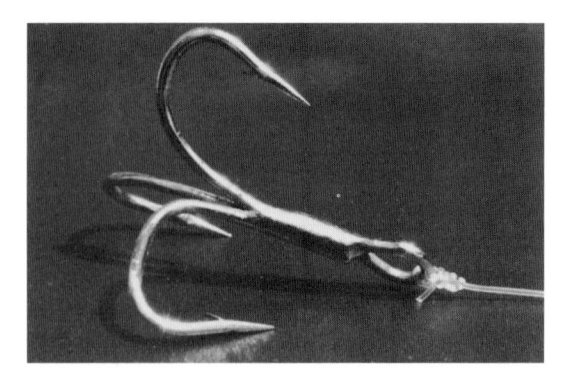

This vicious-looking treble hook was retrieved from the gut of a nine-pounder that had snapped another angler's line.

and is caught again within moments, obviously undeterred by its recent experience. The possibility of fish taking away the rest of the shoal should be considered when returning bass to the sea. Carry them in the weighing sling to a different place – preferably downtide, if possible.

Sometimes the bass are so close you can almost reach out and touch them. Once I was fishing Caldy Island with Brian Harris and Clive Gammon. Brian had just eaten an apple and lobbed the core into the sea. A bass came up and swirled at it. At other times, in flat calm seas, thundery weather has been very kind to me. I recall another time, when Brian fell and broke his ankle while collecting crabs. My friend and I dragged him above the high-water mark, gave him some crabs, and left him to fish. (He insisted on it.) We went off to fish a ledge and had hardly started before a thunderstorm rolled over us with lightning, thunder and torrential rain. I caught four bass. Poor Brian got soaked.

Groundbait is very good for attracting bass and holding their attention. A lone bait provokes only passing interest. In calm seas it is often a good idea partially to bury an open-weave onion sack filled with mackerel guts and chippings in the shingle. It needs to be

WHERE TO FIND BASS INSHORE

weighted down with stones to prevent it drifting away, and it usually draws inquisitive fish to the swim.

Bass regularly hunt at the very edge of the sea, particularly at night. A float-fished bait can prove to be very attractive, but often these circumstances are particularly suited to free-lining. All you need is a rod, a reel and a hook. The bait can be allowed to sink (a small dead mackerel is ideal) or – for more spectacular results – it can be made to float. The 'junkied' pouting is an effective method. It is not necessary, however, to inflate a small dead pouting with a syringe of air; I prefer to jam a piece of polystyrene, shaped like a cigar butt, down the bait's gullet. This works equally well and avoids all the complications and implications of syringes and needles.

Whether the bait is buoyant or not, it is most effective when fished about 3–4ft (1–1.2m) from the edge in calm clear water and preferably out of the tide. If the tide or a side-wind is a problem, some weight will be required. The deadbait can be legered, and the buoyant bait can be fished on a running paternoster, leaving the line slack to allow the bait to float to the surface. Takes are usually violent, with the fish running off some distance before swallowing the bait. The line needs to be able to run freely without over running. A fixed spool is best, as there is no spool inertia to overcome when the fish

Thundery weather is productive: these two seven-pounders were worth getting wet for, and a good reason to keep my eyes on the rod.

WHERE TO FIND BASS INSHORE

moves off with the bait. Because of the intimacy of this method, fish may be scared by lights or by seeing an angler. This trick can be used by day in quiet corners. The trouble is that sea-gulls may pounce on a floating dead fish. At night when they have all flown off to roost, this is unlikely to occur.

I have yet to be convinced that other types of free-lining are particularly successful. I have tried letting baits (both live and dead) drift with the current, but I can't recall achieving anything other than a tangle. Here's what tends to happen. The bait sinks and catches around a weed stem or a rock, where it stops. A lump of drifting weed catches the line and draws it off the reel. Everything seems to be going well until you try to reel in and discover that the line has become a tangle of weeds and knitting. A float or a weight provide much better control of the tackle.

Any appropriate bait can be used for free-lining – even cheese and breadpaste, which have accounted for a surprising number of good fish up to 10lb or more. One angler used to fish two balls of paste on his trace. He let the bass help itself to one then struck when it confidently gulped the other.

Another trick that can be employed from a steep beach, jetty or pier is the slide-down livebait. First, you need to catch the livebait, and usually a second rod is useful for this. A means of keeping the baits alive is also essential, be it a rock pool, a baby's bath or a large aerated bucket of water. Whatever you use, keep it in the shade. The tackle is simplicity itself. Reverse the standard two-swivel tackle. Tie a 4ft (1.2m) lead link or longer to the swivel at the end of the line, and a 2ft (0.6m) hook trace to the running swivel – the one that slides on the line. Catch the hook around one of the rod rings and cast out the weight. The line flows through the swivel without any trouble. Now hook on the livebait and let it slide down the line. The bait is not stressed and stays lively,

Float fishing with live launce from a jetty: the angler caught a three-pounder moments later.

Fishing with floating plugs is highly effective in skinny water over rocks.

WHERE TO FIND BASS INSHORE

My two-swivel rig: complicated end tackle is unnecessary.

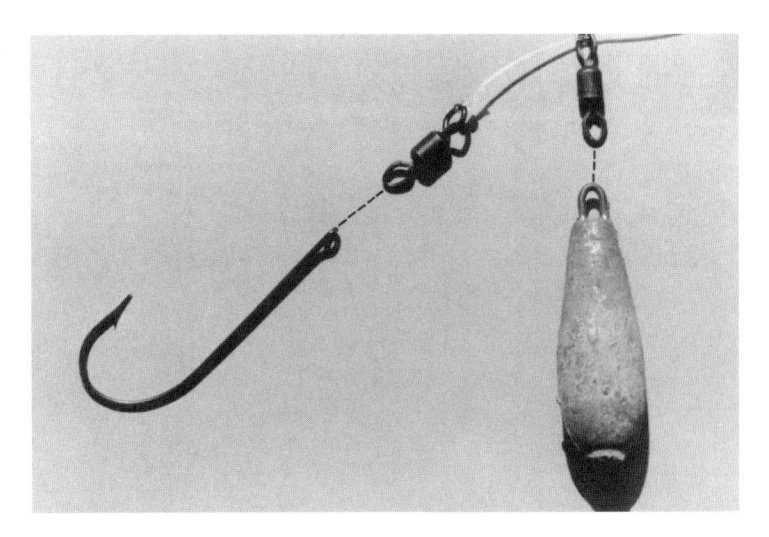

which would not be the case if it were attached to the hook first and then cast out. This trick also works well on piers.

Any warm-water outfall is the bass's equivalent of sunbathing. A lot of good bass, some of them exceedingly large, have been caught from power station outfalls. I once enjoyed a most productive session with Brian Harris and Les Moncrieff, fishing the outfall of the Dungeness Nuclear Power Station. We spent the day casting to the edge of the seething water where bass were hitting the bait (small pouting, sprats and sections of sandeel) so rapidly that, on six consecutive casts, I hooked a fish before the weight hit the bottom. The bass averaged 4–6lbs, but were not really able to put up much of a show on the long-distance casting rods that we were using. We caught about a hundred and put back ninety.

One aspect of shore fishing that should never be denigrated is the fish-in. Members of the Bass Angler's Sportfishing Society organize quite a few each year. When I was younger, my friends and I used to spend long weekends camping beside the seaside and fishing every tide. It is a great way of getting away with a bunch of friends and even better if some decent fish are caught. Travelling around for bass can be great fun, although it rarely yields the best catches. Of course, it is compulsory for anglers who live inland and have to discover hot-spots of their own. The only drawback is the chance of being poisoned by your friends' cooking. I recall that Ian Gillespie used to cook everything in the same pan – eggs, beans, bacon, the lot. The result was usually quite disgusting. I would also advise anglers/campers not to leave valuable tackle lying around while they are away fishing, and make sure that tents are done up tight. We once lost all our food to a party of foxes. Other anglers have lost their tackle to two-footed jackals.

PIERS

Not all piers are open for fishing nowadays. Some are so decrepit that anglers are not allowed onto the lower decks in case a girder collapses and hurts them, or they fall in and drown. Few piers allow night fishing, and several require permits to be bought in advance. You may also need to be a member of a local angling club. How you fish piers depends very much on the depth of water,

WHERE TO FIND BASS INSHORE

the fish-attracting features and how much disturbance they are subjected to by boat traffic and people.

Harbour walls are often productive. The fish swim along the edge, so all you have to do is lower the bait down the side rather than cast it out, unless boulders and concrete blocks are in the way. A drop net is often essential because you can guarantee that when you hook the fish of a lifetime, nobody will be around with a net or to help land your fish. Something like this once happened to me. The only person who could assist me was a Danish student who did not speak any English. He hadn't a clue what I was asking him to do. All he said was 'Yes' and he nodded happily as surges of white water took my fish, tossed it around, and ultimately snapped my line.

Bass generally feed in mid-water around piers that are constructed of girders, and can be caught by using a light lead and allowing the bait to be wafted with the tide under your feet and into the structure. Prawns, ragworms, sandeels and sandeel-shaped strips of mackerel belly are all good baits, fished in a sink-and-draw manner. Takes are usually positive, but often fish have to be held hard to stop them from knitting the line around the girders, cross-braces, tangled trawl nets, barnacle-covered hawsers, and all the other rubbish that collects in such places. Dawn and dusk are usually the best times to have a go for the better fish. Many such piers are home to hordes of bait-nagging schoolies during the day. It is generally a waste of time to cast away from the pier because the fish are inside the structure. It is better to spin a lure along the up-tide edge of the structure, or float fish a prawn, crab or livebait.

Solid piers are like ledges, and the bass sometimes lurk in ambush in front of them, but if the tide is too strong or the structure is too open to create a pocket of still water, the bass can be found in the eddy at the back. On some piers you can see bass sheltering behind the girders – and on the wrecks, too. They show up clearly on the fish finder screen.

I used to fish a small pier and developed a specific method for catching the bass. I tackled up my two swivels with long traces. The lead link was 6ft (2m) long, and the hook link about 9ft (3m) long. The bait was a long strip of squid, pared thin, or a small live pouting. I dropped the weight about 5yds (4.5m) inshore of the end, and about a yard (1m) out. The slim bait caught the tide rushing around the end and fluttered seductively right at the corner. Several bass were caught like that.

ESTUARIES

A warm estuary attracts bass, particularly in spring and late autumn, but cold water deters them. How you fish them depends largely on the size and shape of the estuary. Some are little different in character from the open sea. Bass can be found wherever the by-products of food and fish processing are pumped into the sea. These spots are becoming rarer, however, since the practice of pumping effluent has been banned in some places and is being discontinued in others.

A lot of very good fish are caught from estuaries and harbours on float fished crab, prawn and livebaits, and on lures. Most of these places have sacred corners where people have caught bass for generations, and there is usually a bridge involved somewhere. Judicious trespassing is sometimes necessary, so it helps if your face is known around the harbour or along the waterfront.

The bass generally run the estuary with the flood tide and drop back with the ebb. Some spend days dithering around holding pools up-river, often a long way from the sea and close to fresh water. They probably stay there because they have acclimatized to the lower

WHERE TO FIND BASS INSHORE

Bass come hunting up this gully with the flooding tide, and only a short lob is needed to reach them.

salinity. Bass in pools like this need to be fished for like carp, although they can sometimes be caught on flies, plugs and spinners. They are probably hunting baitfish and are regularly caught on a small float-fished roach or dace. These bass are often quite large, but I find it rather unsettling to see double-figure fish ambling aimlessly around a pool, while cattle graze nearby. They seem to lack the machismo of fish that are caught from the surf and the open sea.

Farther downstream, bass are caught from docksides and other structures, bridges, jetties and in pools below tide-races. They are caught from sand and shingle bars at the mouth of the river, particularly inside larger estuaries, and also on the bars that form a few miles offshore. Bass often shelter inside deep estuaries in stormy weather and big spring tides.

Often the choice of where to fish is limited by practicality, safety, accessibility, ropes, moorings, high-security areas, tall fences, roads and irate officials, but many estuaries offer a microcosm of the coast and the open sea and should be fished accordingly There are scores of them, but I doubt if any two are the same. As ever, find the fish, then find the method.

Float fishing is the method *par excellence* for fishing estuaries, and one of the most successful baits is the live prawn. Bass (and all sorts of fish, like infant pouting), grab a prawn, turn it, and swallow it backwards, with the tail curled in, to avoid the sharp serrated spike at the prawn's head, the rostrum. Perhaps prawns use it to fight off rockling. Bass probably have a way of disabling the prawn before swallowing it. Prawn baits work very well on big spring tides, which encourages more bass to move up-river. Prawns are most active shortly after the tide starts to drain away. It is then easy for a bass to find a vantage point and wait for all the crabs and crustaceans that are drawn back with the ebbing tide. When the water becomes too shallow or dirty, they drop back down the estuary to another vantage point, and then back out to sea.

When the water is clear and bass have found a handy place to ambush bait, they may not move until the tide drains back a long way. They seem to be happy wherever the water is no shallower than the length of the fish.

Bass run small and busy estuaries under cover of darkness when things have quietened down, and they can be caught on prawn, live crab, small pouting, sandeels, and similar bass food. A standard float tackle is fine, with 10 – 15lb line on a carp rod. A reasonable, well-balanced float can be used as hunting bass are much too interested in their prey to bother about the tackle. If it is windy, casting improves

63

WHERE TO FIND BASS INSHORE

A floating dead pout is a deadly method in some places.

if the weight is fished at the end of the line, with the trace coming off above it, paternoster style. The way to do it is to tie the lead link to the trace with a glorified stop-knot, so that the only knot is the one to the hook. These fish are often well into double figures.

An alternative is to fix a bubble float to the line, but this time leave a long trace and tie a little Redgill Rascal on the end, or use a fly rod and the same lure – or a fly. Fly fishing is wonderful in estuaries because the bass gang up on the baitfish and drive them into the current, where they can be easily caught.

Bass can be found in estuaries throughout the season, but lucky is the angler who can find an estuary where small fish like roach, bream and mullet are being washed out to sea by floodwater after a July storm. Most estuaries are like giant hoovers: they suck in a lot of water and inhale all sorts of fry, together with driftwood and rubbish.

Bass run with the tide, and are usually quick off the starting blocks when it floods over a shallow bar to start filling up the estuary. They can be caught almost at your feet as the water rises, but as soon as the waves start washing over the sill, bass are ploughing through the surf to get in there and no more takes are forthcoming. In some places, the bass have a precise awareness of when they can run the river, and turn up just before the water covers the sill. You may get an hour of brilliant sport, then nothing. Often, big fish are caught at night and schoolies by day.

Every estuary has its own times, but the bass only run when they feel a lot of water is coming behind them, and they hunt up the river like a pack of hounds. They mooch lazily around high water and then find bridge supports and other heavy structures where they can ride the ebb and pick off prey. Be it a pier, a shingle bank, pilings, or a ledge, they ride in the slack in front of the obstruction and can see everything the tide brings to them. Towards the end of the tide, they travel back to their starting points, and in some places they stay remarkably close to shore as they move out of the river and along the beach – 20yds (18m) or less.

The most productive way of catching bass in many estuaries is to float fish close to weeds and structure. Bass often swim along the very edge of the water and are likely to miss a bait that has been cast out too far. Prawns and sandeels are excellent baits, but they are as likely to be attacked by mackerel, scad, pouting, pollack and small coalfish as by bass. Float fishing is a fairly selective method because it avoids flounders, crabs and similar vermin.

I often fish with DIY sandeels – long, slim strips of mackerel cut from the flank with a very sharp knife and a cutting board to avoid any ragged edges. These can fish quite well in fast water or when trotting down a swim that has been lightly groundbaited. A slightly underweighted float and a choppy sea make the strip of fish bounce and waft in the water, and induce positive takes. Sandeels are not very easy to come by in my neck of the woods, but we have millions of sprats, which are good baits for trotting a swim. Sandeels have been responsible for some very large catches of bass, usually on the dropping tide over sandbanks or reefs at the estuary mouths. Bass lie in ambush in these places and used to be caught in very large numbers.

WHERE TO FIND BASS INSHORE

Bored and fishless, I wafted it about. I almost had the rod dragged from my hands by a 7lb pollack.

SAFETY

The sea shore is a slippery, dangerous place, so it is always wise to tell friends where you plan to go and when you will be back. Proper footwear and a careful approach are essential at all times. There may be nobody else for miles. On large beaches, a compass is indispensable in case of fog at night.

Tread carefully when walking over weed. The green stuff is treacherous, but there are often spaces between the clumps of bladderwrack where you can put your foot. Muddy pilings and rocks are a hazard, so if the fishing requires any tricky scrambling close to the water, a flotation jacket should be worn, or a life jacket. It is always easier to swim if you do not have to fight to stay afloat at the same time.

Make sure that you have read the tide chart correctly (i.e. the right month!). This will prevent being cut off by the flooding tide. Once you become familiar with your marks, you will discover certain rocks and other marks that indicate the depth of the water. Always leave at the right time. Do not linger for a few minutes more, or you may end up getting cut off by channels

A schoolie is quickly unhooked, to go back and grow bigger and wiser.

Bass have no objection to a float fished peeler, even when it is fairly high above the bottom. If you are fishing from a wall, tuck the bait alongside it (likewise when legering) just on the edge of the weed where it would normally be, but visible to hunting bass. One night, I was float fishing a large edible crab from a wall.

65

WHERE TO FIND BASS INSHORE

It is rarely necessary to cast far to catch bass.

through sand and gullies through rocks. It is amazing how calm and sweet they look at low tide, but when the tide and waves start pouring through, they become raging torrents.

Watch out for mud holes in some places. They're full of slimy clay and as soft as porridge. Never walk out onto piers in rough seas if there is any chance of danger. I was once washed, upright, from one side of a pier to the other. Fortunately the wave expended its power and set me down again with my feet inches from the edge. I think that must have been the sea gods warning me not to be so stupid. Never fish ground by night that you have not explored by day. Fish that are worth catching have been around for many years, and another day – or season – will not make much difference. If in doubt, heed your better judgement, and have a go another time. The bass will have grown bigger by then.

A tide chart and sharp hooks: bare essentials for success.

4 Reefs and Rocks

Reefs and rocks are oases in the sandy desert that provide the bass with shelter and food. The more shelter they offer both bass and food species, the better they are for fishing. A host of small, edible creatures can be found around this sort of structure. You can see this best at night, from a boat in mid-summer. The fish finder screen turns black as everything that has been hiding all day comes out to feed and play. For several yards above the sea-bed, the fish finder shows all sorts of tiny fish, crustaceans and whatever. As dawn comes up, the black blanket on the screen sinks, thins out, and disappears as the workers of the night retire for the day. No doubt they have feasted royally on each other.

Many species of marine life have adapted to sandy beaches, be they the sheltering muddy sort that bass do not really like, or the unstable sandy storm beaches, which they usually frequent. However, in comparison, the rocks teem with life. From the half-tide mark down to 50ft (15m) or more, the surface of every rock is smothered with something growing on it, and this rich food chain extends on up through all the reef fish to the hefty bass that prey on them and – in some places – to the porbeagle sharks that would prey on them. Rock bass have been found to contain mackerel, sandeels, scad, herrings, pouting, poor cod, pollack, small flatfish, wrasse, fifteen-spined sticklebacks, blennies, gobies, pipefish, sprats, and practically every species of crustacean.

Every extensive system of rocks and reefs is visited by bass at some time or another. In more sheltered areas, deeply fissured clay banks are almost as attractive as reefs. Offshore, reefs provide bass with superb

A general rule: the bigger the boulders, the bigger the bass.

REEFS AND ROCKS

ambush places for picking squid and baitfish out of the tide. Large shoals often frequent such areas, and wherever you see a gathering of small fast boats, the commercial anglers are at work. Another give away is a lone boat fishing the same drift for hours on end. When boats are whizzing about all over the sea, nobody has yet found the bass.

Offshore, the bass move from reef to reef according to the supply of baitfish and the strength of the tide, forever turning up where they can breast the current in comfort while their prey is swept past helplessly. Some reef systems may cover 100 square miles (259 hectares) or more with sandbanks, holes and wrecks linking them all together. The bass roam around these areas and regularly turn up in the same place at the same state of the tide, and sometimes on the same days of the year.

Most of these places are the result of centuries of erosion and are backed by cliffs. The rocks and reefs close to shore are an intricate part of the fish's movements and offer the shore angler his best chances of catching a double-figure fish. To give Beachy Head as an example, the bass do not like facing a spring tide in the overfalls offshore and move west and east of the headland to where the current is more temperate. They return to the Head as the tides drop back again.

Consider this: bass weigh the same as water and can either buck the current, go with it, or duck out of it. A one-knot current flows at 1.69 ft per second (fps) (0.5 mps), a two-knot current at 3.38 fps (1 mps), a three-knot current at 5.07 fps (1.5 mps), and a six-knot current, like a big spring through the Menai Strait, is flowing at 10.14 fps (3 mps). Bass are powerful swimmers and can keep station in a fast current, but I do not believe that they prefer being in the main stream to lurking at the edge. It is wonderfully convenient when they drift to the inner edge of a reef with a spring tide. It is also best for gathering peeler crabs and similar delicacies.

Beachy Head ends with a ledge that extends for 2 miles (3km) out to sea, and as the tides increase in strength, some of the fish move closer to shore to take shelter among the rocks rather than gang up elsewhere. The baitfish also consider it safer to take shelter around ledges and rocks closer to shore, and bass have the option of a host of more sedentary rock fish and crustaceans to choose from.

Small bass, up to around 5lbs are much more willing to dash about in a strong tide than big fish are, and in the heyday at Beachy Head, the lunkers were usually caught close to the shore. Sometimes there were dense shoals of them, all very good fish. The big bass, say 8lbs and upwards, cannot be doing with all the rushing around that the juniors get up to and become more sedate and carp-like as they grow older. They are quite capable of catching pouting and mackerel, but they would rather not have to bother too much – a lump of crab-chewed cuttle would be fine. This is probably why very large bass are caught from the rocks in the autumn. They are fat and contented after a summer's feeding and find the conditions to their liking, and titbits easy to catch.

Reefs are usually revealed by overfalls, breaking surf, lobster pot floats, potting boats, charts, and discussions with local fishermen and divers. It is always worth chatting to people who turn up in your swim. They may not be welcome, but they can often tell you what the reef is like out there. The larger and more deeply fissured the reef, the more fish are likely to be around it and sheltering in its shady gullies. They usually move closer to the shore as darkness approaches. A reef that lies 200yds (183m) offshore is likely to supply a run of fish along nearby beaches, particularly if the fish get turfed out of their gullies by rough seas.

As usual, they have exact timetables – when they do turn up. One of the ironies of reef fishing is that the place may be a hot-spot, but

REEFS AND ROCKS

A fine six-pounder, taken on peeler crab from Beachy Head Ledge.

REEFS AND ROCKS

The early morning tide starts to cover a classic bass reef in west Wales.

the flood, and when I catch them from the beach.

Bass can be caught as they return to base after running with the tide or soon after dawn, when they finish their night-time prowling. The middle part of the day is often a good time to catch them around reefs where they have gathered close to shelter or to ambush baitfish. Close to shore, the fish congregate on the lee side of reefs in big tides and rough weather to seek shelter from the current. In weak tides, they prefer the up-tide edge. In clear water, bass come right into the edge of the rocks with the tide, so it is wise to keep out of sight. Don't wade unless the water is especially shallow. One of the best states of tide is when the tide is flooding over weed-beds. The bass are not far behind and as the water deepens, the bigger fish move in.

In dirty water, I have never found rough conditions on shallow reefs to produce as many fish as calm seas. In another place I fish, the water is slightly deeper at 5–6ft (1.5–2m), and it fishes best in choppy conditions. When the water is clear, the fish come into shallow water because surging waves tumble prawns, crabs and small fish out of their hiding places. Surf on rocks appears to be fine if the water is clear or there's a bit of depth.

Cloudy water, with a slight chop, produces the best catches on deadbaits, by day or night. In calm, clear water, a moving bait is much more effective by day and works well at night. Conger eels can sometimes be a problem as they like big edible peelers as much as fish baits, particularly at night. In some places, the early flood can be best for legering, and high water best for spinning or plug fishing.

Bass cruise around shallow reefs looking for what they can scare out and then attack with scorching acceleration. They sometimes ground themselves on kelpy rocks in their enthusiasm to seize baitfish and can often be seen swirling and splashing at the edge. Big

you may not get a bite. You may have been fishing the wrong method, or at the wrong state of the tide, or the wrong time of year, or the fish may not be there on that particular tide. It is nothing unusual to have a good catch and return to the same place with high hopes, only to end up fishless.

One of my favourite reefs fishes well from the boat as darkness falls and the tide starts running. I fish about 150yds (137m) out from the beach. Everything goes well for a while, then shuts off. That is precisely when the fish turn up inshore, about two hours into

REEFS AND ROCKS

atmospheric pressure. The tide on some ledges changes before the published time. At Beachy Head the flood starts half an hour before the time given in the tide chart. It is odd to watch boats farther offshore still streaming on their anchor rope with the ebb tide.

Rock fishing is great fun for the shore angler, as success can be had at any time of day or night in mid-summer. You can go for miles, alone or with a friend, and spend an entire day exploring the coast line and casting here and there. It helps to carry tackle and kit in a ruck-

I find calm seas are most productive when reef fishing with crab.

grey mullet swimming indolently around the rocks can give good impersonations of bass.

Before you start fishing, find an easy place to land the bass. Usually they can be slid up a gully or into a rock pool without any difficulty, but deeper bouldery water requires a net. Never help them ashore with your boot, lest you get spiked on a dorsal fin.

You should always watch the tide and note which rocks are covered when the first fish takes. This is more reliable than the tide chart, which is not always accurate. Tides may be delayed or accelerated by high winds and

When rock fishing, a convenient gully can usually be found for landing bass.

71

REEFS AND ROCKS

Rock bass bite freely by day when the water has been clouded by rough seas.

sack, as it leaves at least one hand free for scrabbling and makes things easy to carry, especially if a long journey is in prospect. Shoulder bags put you off-balance and have a habit of sliding round awkwardly at tricky moments, like when negotiating an overhang.

I always refer to a checklist of what to take with me so that important items of tackle are not left behind. A last-minute glance down the list has often saved me time and frustration. More than a few anglers have walked miles to fish a lonely hot-spot in perfect conditions only to discover that their reel, hooks, bait or elastic thread have been left behind. For early-morning starts, get everything organized the night before.

REEFS AND ROCKS

BOTTOM FISHING

The more snaggy the swim, the more likely you are to catch bass. However, several weights, hooks, and traces are liable to be lost so it pays to have spare sets made up, so that you can retackle and cast out quickly before the fish move on. You can use a standard bass rod or a carp rod, depending on the tactics you intend to use. I usually fish with 30lb line on the reel because one good swipe across a flint reduces it to 8lb. Tackle sometimes needs to be quite heavy in extremely graunchy swims, and quite a heavy lead, perhaps 5–6oz (142–170g), may be needed to contend with the strongest tides.

Spark plugs can be used as weights, and are readily available from garages, but most times they are horribly oily, and I doubt that bass like finding the smelly things lying near a bait. I much prefer lightweight bombs, weighing ¾–2oz (21–57g). I do not mind losing weights, although it is nicer to reel them back again. Lead is cheap enough and hundreds can be made in one session, especially if somebody gives a helping hand. Fortunately, hooked bass usually lift the lead off the bottom while they are fighting.

Heavy line is often essential, ending with a running leger or paternoster. The trace needs to be about 16lb (7kg), and I prefer a rotten bottom of about 6lb (3kg) to a lighter sinker. A leader is anathema because that means everything is lost to a snag. A short trace is best in surfy, rolling tides. Long traces and light weights are best in calm, settled conditions with little tide, but crabs may drag the bait under a rock and snag it.

Many rock marks have convenient holes and boulders that can be used as a rod rest, or can be made into a rod rest by positioning a small boulder to hold the butt down should a fish lunge at the rod top. However, rod rests encourage laziness, and bites are often missed. None the less, they are convenient when fish are not yet expected in the swim.

A cool-bag is handy for frozen baits in hot weather. The shore line gets very hot when

A selection of small bombs for rock fishing, ¾–2oz (21–57g).

REEFS AND ROCKS

the sun is reflecting off the cliffs. I prefer to gather crabs prior to fishing, even when I am in my boat. I gently nose into a wide gully or bay and throw the anchor ashore on the upwind side so that the boat drifts into open water on the end of its tether. It is important to know the lie of the boulders lest the prop gets damaged.

Crab is the bait *par excellence* for rock fishing, and many anglers tuck their peeler alongside edges of the reef or beside a boulder. Lugworm is useless from the rocks: reef-dwelling species make the best baits. If wrasse and pouting continuously rip crab baits apart, it is best to fish with a wrasse or pouting as they are not cannibals. Strongly scented baits are necessary in cloudy water, especially after a storm when the bass return to the rocks after the water and weed have cleared and fishing becomes practical again.

Fish are often very close in. Once, on a camping and fishing weekend with Brian Harris, Ian Gillespie and Doug Cooper, they helped themselves to the bait from my bucket and spread out along the rocks in front of a shallow gully. I was compelled to waste part of the tide gathering more crabs, and as they had already taken the best positions, I had to fish in the gully behind them, and stare at their backs. It struck me as daft until I started to get bites. I caught the only bass, a four-pounder. The mouth of a wide gully is often one of the best places to fish.

In a strong lateral tide, the fish may be within a few yards of your feet, so short casts are often best. They also limit the number of

A bare minimum of tackle is necessary when fishing the rocks with peeler crab.

REEFS AND ROCKS

Late evening fishing over a reef with crab.

snags you have to bring the tackle back over. There is no point casting far over shallow reefs and then losing fish to snags. I cast the minimum distance and then tighten the line incompletely, so that it is slightly slack. Never give the bait a pull to ensure that it is not snagged as this usually drags it into a snag.

The best way to detect bites is to point the rod down the line and feel for the take. Hold a loop of line and watch where it enters the sea. Often you see it jerk, with a slight 'V' wake, as the fish picks up the bait. I lean forward and hold the rod out in front of me to give the fish some slack. Generally, I fish with the reel out of gear, in case the fish wants a lot of line. Usually everything suddenly comes up

REEFS AND ROCKS

tight and the fish can be struck. If it doesn't, lean back again and gently take up the slack to find out what has happened. In calm water, with no current, I often leave the line fairly slack and watch where it enters the water. I love to see that rippling 'V' wake as the line tightens. It is very exciting.

Bites are always positive where a shoal of bass is working around structure, but in these days of depleted stocks, there is less competition between individual bass. Takes can be very gentle and may take a while to develop. A large bass may dither around with a bait for several minutes before taking it, and even then may take it very gently. You have to evaluate all the taps and plucks, and decide when to show your hand. I usually strike, reel the line up tight again, and then strike once again to ensure that the hook is firmly home. Do not over do this, however. You do not want to pull its head off.

When reeling in to check the bait, I lean forwards with the rod pointing down the line, strike, and reel like crazy to bring the tackle over the top of the snags. If this fails and the tackle snags, do not strike hard at the snag with the rod lest you snap the tip. Point the rod down the line, with the reel spool stopped from slipping, and walk steadfastly backwards until something gives. Care is also needed when hauling plugs, spinners and lead weights out of weeds. They may fly back and catch you in the face. Once I had a weight crack off behind me as the tackle flew clear, and it hit the cliff 60yds (55m) away. Do it sideways and make sure nobody is in the way.

A fighting bass often kites away to one side, and side-strain with the rod is necessary to turn a rapidly departing fish and prevent it from snagging the line around a rock. This is sometimes necessary when fighting a large fish. The bigger bass stay deep, and do not fight in the splashy manner of smaller fish.

I often fish reefs from my boat, sometimes parking it close to the shore line. The boat permits me to use a longish trace – about 4ft (1.2m) – as it fishes straight down the tide. The boat is also ideal for fishing into a trail of groundbait, either chopped mackerel or crushed crabs. This method produces a good number of fish, but sometimes the best groundbait trail yields no bass, although that is often due to the weather. Groundbait is handy anywhere, and it can be thrown into your swim from the shore with a 'magapult' (a catapult designed for hurling out maggots).

Reefs are much easier to fish from the boat because there is scant risk of slipping over and breaking an ankle. However, absolute silence is essential, with no banging about. Calm water is best as it does not slap against the hull. I usually throw the groundbait up beyond the prow of the boat so that it sinks before it reaches my swim, which is usually about 30yds (27m) behind the boat. This is a wonderful trick on a calm evening, as dusk comes in. I sit and listen to the kittiwakes squealing incessantly along the cliffs and groups of fulmars paddling in circles beside the boat, angrily debating the issues of the day, and then… was that a tap?

FLOAT FISHING

Float fishing is a rock and reef technique, although it usually works best in clear water. It is ideal for fishing the rough water at the mouth of a deep gully, where the waves are swirling around the crabs, prawns and small fish. It is also a handy method where bass wait in ambush among reefs alongside channels, or in channels through reefs, and of course, it keeps the bait out of reach of snags.

The float should be nicely balanced by the weight so that the fish feel little resistance when they take the bait. This is achieved by using the minimum size of float that can be cast out to the swim and presents the bait effectively. It needs to be large enough to be visible in a choppy sea and not be dragged under by wave action. In snaggy swims, I use floats cut from lengths of polythene foam with a swivel tied at the bottom. A float that cocks nicely to a ½oz (14g) drilled bullet is usually adequate, but much lighter floats can be used in sheltered areas where the bass are likely to be put off by resistance and reject the bait.

Most of the time, a sliding float is best so that the depth at which the bait fishes can be adjusted as the water deepens. All you need is a small bead on the line and a moveable stop-knot. Often the bait can be fished very close to shore, to keep everything under control, but beware of scaring the fish when the water is clear.

Float fishing is a visually appealing method of fishing, and the bass usually grab the bait and go, without messing around with it. The method is very sporting because lighter line can be used, together with a carp rod. You can use the wind and tide effectively to explore a lot of ground.

A fairly long trace is best as it allows the bait to waft around seductively. Baits can be live crisp crabs or peelers, or bundles of dead crab. Bass do not look askance when they find a dead crab bouncing around beneath a float. The old method was to poke the eye of a treble hook through the crab from beneath, and then loop the line onto it, but I detest treble hooks for bait fishing.

Movement is essential to attract the attention of the fish, and to suggest that the bait is swimming under its own steam. Long, slim fillets of mackerel, squid, and launce are all suitable, hooked once through one end. Prawns work very well, either singly if they are large, or in bunches if they are small. Lively ragworms are also effective, fished in bunches if they are small. The bass usually strike any small live fish quite violently.

This tiny promontory has yielded many bass over the years. They hunt through the gullies 30yds (27m) out.

Another highly effective method is to anchor up-tide of a rock and trot a float-fished livebait over the top of the rocks. The bass are usually hunting small fish, and a boat is very handy for keeping the bait alive. Some distance may be covered, so the float needs to be readily visible. One trick is to make a float out of old wine bottle corks and a strip of bamboo cane (available from any garden centre, stained dark green). A tiny swivel is fixed to

REEFS AND ROCKS

the lower end, and dart flights are glued to the top. They can be seen from a long way.

A similar technique can be used when live-baiting around the rocks and concrete blocks on the outside of harbour walls. The bass take refuge in caves inside these walls, and usually come out to feed at dusk unless shoals of bait-fish lure them into the open. A boat is usually a much safer platform than a slippery lump of concrete.

LURE FISHING

Lure fishing is dealt with more extensively later on, in its own chapter. However, shore fishermen should always be alive to the presence of livebait and the opportunities for lure fishing that they present. Shoals of baitfish are sometimes driven out of their rocky refuges below the low-water mark and are pushed inshore of reefs and piles of boulders. Here, a short cast is most likely to catch them, particularly if there are lanes of clear water inshore of the reefs and cloudy water offshore.

One problem with very large reefs inshore is that the bass can spread out over them. Offshore, feeding bass are nearly always some distance up-tide of the reef or along the up-tide edge, where they congregate to ambush baitfish. Usually the angler has to discover the exact slot where bass are prepared to take a lure. Inshore, this usually shifts closer with the tide.

SAFETY

Some rock marks can only be reached with proper rock-climbing equipment and should not be attempted by the inexperienced. There is rarely much point in fishing dangerous areas because the bass probably swim past them on their way to a much more accessible place at a different state of tide.

Rocks are hard, immovable objects that snap bones and bruise you. Never rush around, but take it easy and plan your footing before taking the next step. Mistrust damp green weed, and do not step on sloping rocks unless absolutely necessary. Try to avoid jumping from rock to rock unless they offer a solid grip or are covered with barnacles. Always watch out for slimy weed, especially when the tide covers a smooth-bottomed rock pool.

Note the state of tide when certain rocks cover. It is a reliable guide for when to quit and get back before being cut off. Watch out for deep gullies and headlands that may block your retreat. Beware of being cut off.

If the rocks lie in deeper water and the occasional growling swell sometimes sweeps over them, wear a life jacket and make sure there is something to hang on to, even if that means banging a spike into a fissure and fixing a rope to it. Rough seas on some reefs are very dangerous. Reflect that if you do not take risks, you will live to fish another day.

Watch out for falling rocks when you are under cliffs. Huddling close to them is dangerous. Recently an angler had a lucky escape just down the road from me. A cliff fall happened while he was walking past. The blast lifted him off his feet and threw him into the sea. Sadly, his dog was killed. The softer and less stable the cliff, the greater the chance of lumps falling off it. Chalk is very dodgy, but granite and hard sandstone are less likely to bounce boulders off your skull.

Wading in rocky areas is dicey, especially if you cannot see the bottom through cloudy seas or where the rocks shelve steeply. Wading is often essential when returning to dry land, and a route can easily be planned in advance. Take the reel off your rod and use it as a wading staff to feel the bottom. That is another good reason why a bass rod requires a bit of back-bone.

5 Baits

One of the joys of bass fishing is that the fish know precisely what they want. They either ignore the bait completely, or gulp it down. The intermediate stage of having a go even though they are not interested is infrequent, although that is often due to bait presentation or the method in use.

This generosity applies earlier in the year, before the bass have become well fed. Late in the season, when they become fat and torpid, takes are often half-hearted unless the bait is presented so precisely that the fish have to exert themselves very little to eat it. This usually occurs as they approach their pre-spawning period. They reach a point where most humans would be saying to their family or spouse 'I think I ought to go on a diet'.

After a rich summer feeding, and full of fat, the bass start feeling bloated and rarely look at a bait unless it is an easy catch. While

For some reason velvet swimmers are abundant around here.

BAITS

preparing to fatten their roes, bass spend very little energy on pursuit. Some of the females will be having more than 2 million children within a few months and some of the big males will be capable of of fathering many more. By this time, water temperatures are dropping rapidly away from their mid-summer high, and an easily caught herring can provide nourishment for the best part of a fortnight. During the cold months, the bass go on a diet. Digestion slows down, and the growing roes take up space in the body cavity and reduce space for the stomach, which is already restricted by fat.

When the bass reach this state of torpor, anglers call it a season, but the fish are wide open to the predations of trawlers which scoop up scores of tons of them before they have had the opportunity to spawn. However, from May through to October, the bass often go on the rampage. They have one, simple philosophy: go to the head of the queue, and eat the best there is. That is how they pack on fat so fast. Remember that everything that is not too big to eat them is eyed up as a potential meal, and they have the speed to guarantee it. It is their instinct to feed, grow fat, and multiply. That is all they ever want to do, and that is why they are caught in such a diversity of places and on such a wide variety of baits.

Bass are such opportunists that you could provide a spread of delicious baits, like the menu of a first-class restaurant, and they would eat four starters and five main courses – if they felt hungry and safe. Bass have an in-built sense of self-preservation and are quick to drop a bait that seems to be attached to something else, particularly when they have the time to nose around it, smell the rust on the hook, the rubber in the elastic thread, and no doubt the diesel, garlic pâté and tobacco that were on the angler's hands while he was preparing his offering.

Fish have a highly sensitive sense of smell. It is so precise that it enables species like salmon to locate the stream where they were spawned. As for bass, I reckon that if salmon are clever enough to sniff out their grandmother's birthplace from 2,000 miles (3,200km), they can detect any suspicious or unpleasant scent on a bait from 2in (5cm). I always wash my hands before baiting up for bass. On many occasions I have fished with friends and have caught fish after fish, while they caught little more than an apology. Somewhere along the line, good habits pay dividends, and when one angler consistently catches more than the others, scent is quite possibly a contributory factor.

This brings us to the nitty-gritty of all angling. We can only think like fish up to a certain point. After that, we must rely on reasonable conjecture. In the broader spectrum, such as working out where to fish, that can pay tremendous dividends, but on the narrow scale, who really knows what a bass actually sees and feels as it approaches or attacks a bait? To find that out, scientists will have to wire up a bass's brain to a computer that can interpret its thoughts and project them as virtual reality. No doubt machines like this will be widely available in toy shops by Christmas, but until then, anglers will have to go by their own instincts.

Bass eat many of the marine species that are sold as seafood: squid, fish, prawns, edible crabs and the like. The vast majority of bass are caught on baits that are so fresh and juicy that you could eat them yourself. Congers readily accept baits that are long past their sell-by date, but bass prefer their prey to be alive or at the very least still bleeding. If it is so fresh that it is still twitching, so much the better. I am well aware that certain holiday-makers on the pier catch monsters on slices of stale mackerel shaped like fish-fingers, but proficient bass anglers catch many more by being crafty.

BAITS

Ever since I have been fishing for bass, I have learnt that bass are sometimes very much aware of the possibility that a bait may be attached to something nasty, like an angler. Obviously there are times when the bass roar off with the bait and are easy to hook, but sometimes a fish can be felt picking up the bait, then dropping it. It does not come back, nor does it take your friend's bait. It felt something strange, was spooked, and vacated the area.

A perfect bait on its own does not catch fish; it has to be correctly prepared, properly mounted onto the hook, and fished skilfully. Even when a fish drops the bait, there is the empty satisfaction of knowing that part of the equation proved to be successful.

I had a little laugh when I reread 'correctly prepared' in that last paragraph, because the best way to prepare some baits is to smash them up, so that the juices flow. In the context of bass fishing this is 'correctly prepared' because the fish tend to travel fast along the shore line or wherever else they are feeding, and a juicy bait emits a strong scent trail that is likely to entice a fish. Plenty of prey gets smashed up by rough seas and trawlers, so a bait that is almost too badly lacerated to be recognizable is perfectly normal.

Precision casting can be beneficial when bass are around in any numbers, particularly where they tend to move through fast. Blood and other bits linger where a bait once was, and, during the fight a juicy bait will have been pulverized, releasing a strong scent trail. I am a firm believer in rebaiting as fast as possible and getting the bait back out to the same place. Another bass may already be nosing up the gully where the bait was lying before the last fish was hooked. Bass are so often in your swim for such a brief spell, that it makes sense to have baits ready prepared. You can hook and land three fish in the same time it takes another angler to catch only one.

Few bass can resist a lovingly prepared peeler crab.

Bass will grab hold of anything edible at any time, should the opportunity present itself, but from the angler's point of view, baits fall into two categories: those that appeal through scent, and livebaits that appeal through sight and possibly vibration. However, no bait will ever convince a bass unless it matches the sea-bed round about. Some baits work best in certain contexts, and bass can be highly discerning when a bait is out of context. Of course, they eat odd things at times, but we bass anglers prefer to keep our feet firmly planted in probability rather than experimenting with the surreal concoctions that preoccupy carp fishermen.

Match fishermen often use fiddly baits to catch small fish and build up their weight during a competition, but this book is not about how to win matches by catching barely

BAITS

sizeable school bass. It is about sport fishing for a species that has a rumbustious appetite, and the bigger specimens are most frequently caught on large helpings of bait.

Although the size of the bait matters quite a lot, its shape is important too. It needs to be shaped so that a bass will have little trouble picking it up and taking it into its mouth. The more it has to pick it about and juggle it before trying to swallow it, the more likely the fish will be to feel resistance on the line, become suspicious, and drop the bait.

Anglers frequently talk about fish being hungry, and so they are at times. However, bass are usually surrounded by crabs and baitfish and are never desperate to take an angler's offering at any price. If it is not right or they feel the rod tip, they will invariably exercise a judicious refusal.

CRABS

Bass readily eat crabs at any time of the year. There are several species for them to hunt within 2 miles (3km) of the shore, and crab would probably be quite a good bait far beyond the horizon, although I have yet to try it out there. In June I have often caught bass containing masked crabs from offshore wrecks. They are a small species that is found in deep water.

In May, June and into July, the bass are regathering their strength after spawning, and crabs provide them with a square meal. Crabs are not hard to catch and are sometimes extremely abundant at a time when the sea is still warming up after winter and the fish are not exerting themselves too much. It is one of nature's generous coincidences that crabs

A peeler velvet swimming crab (left) and an edible crab (right) make ideal baits for reef fishing.

moult their shells and become semi-defenceless when the bass need a nutritious diet.

Bass eat plenty of hard crabs, but they have to attack and subdue them. Defenceless peelers and softies are more easy to catch and also make effective baits. Sometimes crabs moult in such profusion that it seems as though there are not enough crevices for them all. They can be found in the most inadequate of hiding places, and the bass have little trouble catching their share. Consequently, it is often a good idea to fish over the same ground where the crabs have collected.

A crab has to moult its shell to increase in size. Different species moult at different times of the year, and the timing of this varies around the coast. As a crab reaches its time, it absorbs nutrients from its old shell, making it feel soapy and smooth. The shell looks old and faded, and many crabbers can differentiate between hard backs and 'peelers' just by the colour of the shell. This, however, can vary around the country – probably due to minerals in the water – and what looks like a perfect peeler in one place can turn out to be a solid hard back elsewhere. Shore crabs generally have a pronounced orange tinge on their undershell when they are ready to moult.

Eventually, a crack forms around the back of the shell and the crab crawls backwards out of its old suit of clothes, discarding everything hard from its old shell – stomach lining, eyes, gills, the lot. It then pumps itself full of water to expand the soft, new shell. Moulting can only take place in water. After a few hours the shell becomes crisp as it starts to harden. Once this stage is completed, the crab returns to being its normal cantankerous shelf. As it feeds, it grows inside its new shell until that, in turn, becomes too cramped and the process begins again. As a general rule, small crabs moult three or four times during the summer, but large crabs may moult once.

The bass angler can fish with total confidence when the rock pools are littered with cast-off shells. When this happens, bass are not far away and are enjoying a bonanza of easy pickings. Sometimes a soft crab is found sitting alongside its cast-off shell, which is usually about half its size. A recently shed shell looks like a dead crab, but it should open up easily to reveal shreds of mucus and clean, creamy coloured gills. If they are black, bacteria has started to decompose them and the crab is long gone. If the old shell still looks fresh, there is every chance that the soft crab is close by. Depending on the species, it may be under a nearby rock or fringe of weed. As a general rule, soft crabs move down the shore after moulting, keeping in the water. If they

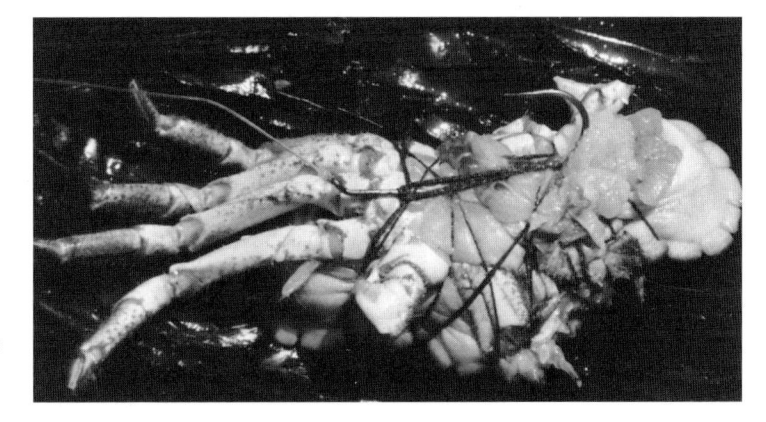

A perfect peeler edible crab. There is no need to hide the hook, and the legs on one side ensure the bass takes the bait hook first.

BAITS

are in a land-locked pool, they can normally be found at the seaward end.

Besides general colour, feel, and cracks around the shell, the easy way to tell a peeler from a hard back is by breaking the tip off one of the legs. This is harmless, and if the crab has scant intention of peeling, the damage will heal at the next moult. If it is not a peeler, jelly and sinews will be revealed, but if it is a peeler, the shell will come away cleanly revealing a fresh new leg. It should end with a perfectly formed toenail. Crabs frequently lose legs and claws, and often one is found with a soft limb. These crabs usually turn out to be peelers.

Sometimes two crabs are found together, the larger one on top carrying the smaller one underneath. Crabs can only mate when the hen is soft, so the underneath one is always a hen. The cock carries her the right way up prior to peeling, them turns her upside down and mates with her when she is soft and crisping up again. In spring, the cocks peel first, so it is easy to see by a glance at the apron whether to test if a crab is a peeler. Hen crabs only peel when mating. Shortly after the spring flush, the carriers appear. Should you find a pair of edible crabs, the cock is often big enough for the pot.

It is a matter for speculation, but hen crabs sometimes seem to make better baits than cocks. It has been suggested that the hen releases a pheromone, a chemical messenger, to which the cocks respond. If this is the case, it is highly probable that the bass are aware of it. The way to sex a crab is to turn it upside down and inspect its apron. This is the vestigial tail tucked between its legs. Hens have a broad apron, shaped like a shield, which is used for holding the eggs. The apron of cocks is narrow and pointed, like a spear.

The way to gather crabs is to pull on a pair of waders and go hunting for them. A large bucket is needed, preferably one with a broad base so that it doesn't topple over and dump the captives back into the sea. The first thing I do is put several clumps of bladderwrack weed into the bucket. The crabs can burrow into the weed and take shelter, which helps to keep them calm.

Soft crabs and peelers do not mix. This is particularly the case with edible crabs, which embrace anything that their claws come into contact with, be it weed or other crabs. The solution is to separate the soft from the others so that they do not get damaged. I do this by putting them at the bottom of the bucket, under the weed. Some anglers use a square bucket or box and make a partition across the middle with plywood, but I have yet to feel the need for such a container.

Shore Crabs

Shore crabs are abundant throughout the British Isles and can be found anywhere between the open sea and the upper reaches of estuaries. In summertime, they are the first crabs to peel, which makes them a reliable bait for the early season. In Sussex, the cock shore crabs also peel fairly abundantly in early autumn, when they are known locally as 'jack-apples'. However, shore crabs have a slightly bitter smell, and many bassmen are convinced that velvet swimmers and edible crabs are more appetizing and make superior baits.

Water temperature is one of the keys to what makes crabs peel (it may have something to do with day length, but no crab has yet confessed, even under torture). Early in the season, estuaries and creeks warm up faster than the open sea, and the first collectable peeler shore crabs can be found in even the tiniest backwaters and warm marshland drains from mid-March onwards. Much depends on how warm and sunny the weather is, and whereabouts in Britain you are looking. This is best discovered through local enquiries. It is important to note the times of the year

BAITS

Shore crabs stay alive for a long time if they are given a regular drink of fresh sea water.

when crabs peel in profusion in your locality so that bait gathering and fishing expeditions can be planned to coincide with them.

Peeler shore crabs can be found somewhere in Britain throughout the year and are shipped up from the West Country in winter. I have found small ones in my part of the world in January, so they would seem not to be worried about how cool the weather is. If there is any chance of catching a bass, why not gather some shore crabs and have a go.

There is a risk of being more keen than the bass and fishing empty water, with perhaps the chance of a schoolie. As soon as the weather warms up, some anglers are so overcome by enthusiasm that they devastate the crabbing marks, desperate for the smallest of baits, and mess up the place before the first shoal of the season comes hunting along the shore line. A certain amount of restraint is required because a few weeks of sunshine are essential before the sea warms up enough to

My crab crusher is ideal for converting hard backs into groundbait.

BAITS

start the ball rolling. In the old days, we often caught decent cod and a few bass from the rocks when the shore crabs started peeling, but that pleasure has long since been denied to sport fishermen.

I always look forward to a long season, with about a hundred days when chances are good for catching bass, but feeding activity starts at 10°C (50°F), and does not speed up until 13°C (55°F). The sea warms up a bit more each day, but even so it is usually a couple of weeks before the fish show any consistency. I am content to let somebody else catch the first fish of the season. They are usually very slender and lack the depth of bass in late July. Of course, quite a few early bass are ten-pounders that go on to spend long summer days pigging out on baitfish and squid, and can turn the scales at 12lb (5kg) when they make their way back in the autumn.

I know it is asking for a miracle and that anglers are not always the ones to blame, but it would be nice if people were to put back rocks, crocks, and other crab-attracting structure in exactly the same place where they found them. All too often, rocks are thoughtlessly toppled over, burying the weed away from the sunlight so that it rots and stinks. This also exposes the multitude of organisms that have spent millions of years living under rocks to bright sunlight, churning seas and drying winds. Put back the rock carefully, and sooner or later another crab will take its place. Topple it over, and the crabs will moult elsewhere.

'Crabitat' is precious. Some rocks, holes and pools are much more likely to hold peelers or soft crabs than others, so they should be carefully maintained and where possible enhanced. Nothing can dig its way under a buried rock, but we often heave them up, just in case. If a few large stones are put into the hole before rolling it back, a peeler will probably show its appreciation before too long. For many years it has been the practice in the West Country to spread ridge tiles and all sorts of rubble around estuaries, offering homes to wandering peelers. Most of these are commercial enterprises, and visitors would be ill-advised to tamper with them.

Peeler shore crabs are found in saltmarsh creeks, under rubble, inside part-buried car tyres, under weeds, tight against walls and breakwaters, and in every other nook and cranny that holds a bit of water. Sometimes they are in the silt at the bottom of a tiny muddy pool. Peelers can be found in shallow creeks, estuaries and backwaters several weeks before they are abundant in sun-warmed rock pools along the open shore. Shore crabs are not great diggers, so it is not uncommon to find swarms of them under large rocks halfway down the shore. So few of these have ever turned out to be peelers that I no longer bother to catch them – except for groundbait.

Edible Crabs

Edible and velvet swimming crabs do not have the bitter pungency of shore crabs. While preparing them for bait, one cannot fail to notice the much more attractive scent and the amount of thick juice that they have. Bass frequently show a preference for these rather than shore crabs, and I have often caught several good fish when other anglers fishing alongside with shore crabs have not had a bite. Time and time again, I have cast out one of these perfect baits and had it taken almost immediately. They simply taste better. Both edible and velvet swimming crabs taste delicious when cooked, but I have yet to see shore crabs on any seafood stall in France – or anywhere else. The minimum takeable size for edibles is 5½in (14cm), but nobody has told the bass that.

Edible crabs are found among reefs, rocks and rubble on open shore lines, close to the low water mark. They are diggers, and tunnel under rocks, rafts of mussels and ledges. These

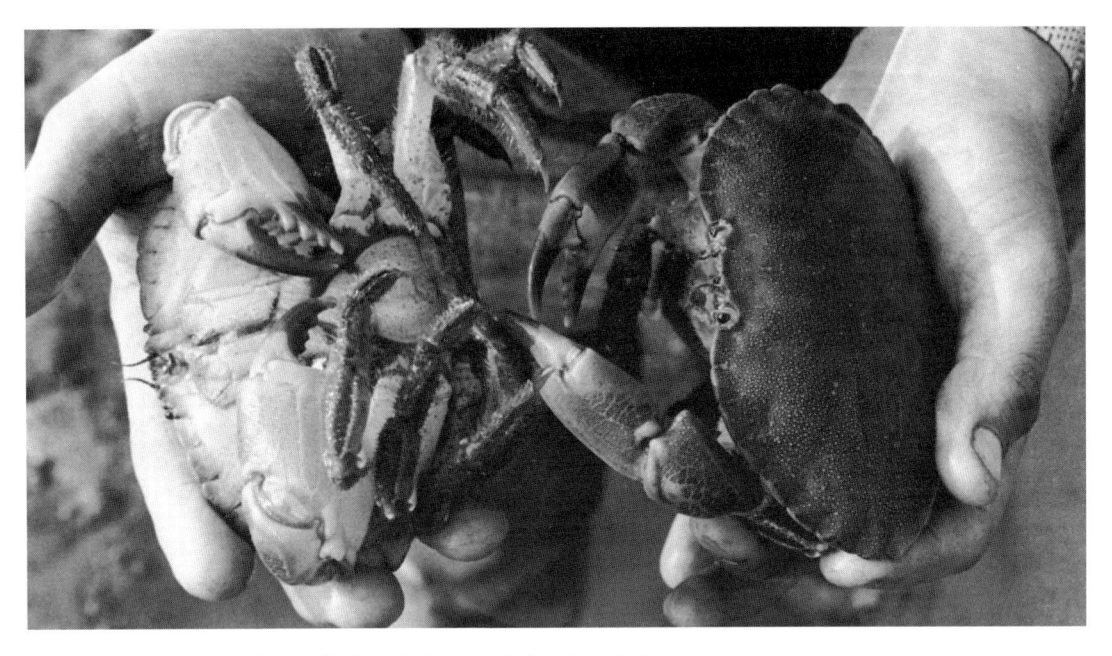

Crisp edible crabs can be peeled again for a soft, luscious bait.

excavations often reveal their position. Like all crabs, the smallest peel first, followed by the bigger ones. Happy is the man who finds a carrying couple because both may be big enough for the pot. It is worth putting an old onion sack in your pocket if big edibles are around. They can often be found in the same holes season after season. The sack tangles them up and keeps them quiet. Otherwise, they would make a dreadful mess of the bucket's occupants.

Most edible peelers are found buried in sand and gravel in a tiny pool under a large rock. You sometimes have to trawl through the sand for them with your finger tips, which does nothing for the nails. Some people use gloves. When groping under rocks and around the back of crevices, it is impossible to feel what angle a crab is lying at. This is essential in order to catch it before it retreats into an inaccessible cranny. I do not use gloves, and grit my teeth each time a rock slips from my grasp and the barnacles gouge my fingers.

Sometimes the crab has backed under a flat stone beneath the main rock. Peelers have no wish to be found, so they do their best to hide away and camouflage themselves from view. They have to be hunted for – by day or night. I have been crabbing by lamplight and by moonlight. Sometimes the rocks are in knee-deep pools, but in my experience few edible peelers are found under them. One problem is that as soon as you heave up the rock, silt clouds the water. Nothing can be seen, and the crabs escape.

Edibles can also be found at the back of crevices and small caves. I once found peelers in crevices in the walls of quite a large cave. The way to evict a crab from a deep crevice is to grab a claw and pull the crab sideways. The trick is to take it by surprise, then grab the legs and pull it out before it can consolidate its position against further attack. Fortunately

BAITS

edible crabs aren't swift in self-defence, but they can trap an unwary hand against the rock. Watch out for their claws at all times – they are very powerful. Some people use a strong metal hook to drag them out, others take sledgehammers and crowbars to the rocks, but that is not environmentally sensitive behaviour.

Bait collecting is often as much fun as fishing. Every flat rock with a gap under one edge seems to call out 'Lift me!'. It is easy to forget the time and miss the bass that run through with the first flush of the tide, although your back muscles are usually screaming for a rest by then.

Severe damage can be done to your back if you try to lift enormous rocks, especially if they are still firmly planted in the earth's crust. Here is how to do it. First find the easiest angle for lifting the rock and, if necessary, remove small boulders and other obstructions. Stand with one leg each side of the rock so that they are out of harm's way should it topple over. Bend the knees, take a firm grip of the rock, clench the stomach muscles, keep the back straight, and lean backwards, pushing with the legs until the rock reaches its point of balance.

Velvet Swimming Crabs

Mercifully, velvet swimming crabs do not demand nearly as much exertion. They sometimes make scrapes under rocks, but do not dig themselves in like edible crabs. They are to be found under rocks, beneath ledges, in rock pools and other generally accessible places. The minimum takeable size is 2½in (6.5cm).

A soft velvet swimming crab alongside its old shell.

They often gather in large numbers to moult and in quite a small area. My favourite stretch of shoreline for catching them is about 250yds (230m) long. This is probably due to the nature of the ground in that area, which consists of narrow gullies, ledges, boulders and bladderwrack. On several occasions I have found two or three perfect baits under one rock.

Velvet swimmers, which are also known as 'whifflers' or 'fiery Freds', are very dependent on water. Both softies and peelers die quickly unless the bucket contains cool, aerated sea water, and even then they are hard to keep alive. They are often found in long, narrow pools, but not ones that are spring-fed with fresh or brackish water. The easiest way to flush them out is to stand in the pool and shuffle to the seaward end, trying not to disturb the silt. The velvet swimmers can be seen gliding away, looking as menacing when soft as they are when hard. The difference is that the softies carry their claws tight to their body while peelers and hard backs carry them aloft, spoiling for a fight. As these claws are very sharp and swimmers are very agile, bait collectors should stay alert. Most of these narrow pools end with a boulder or lump of rock at the seaward end. The velvet swimmer is often found sheltering beneath it, particularly if a freshly shucked shell has been seen lying at the bottom of the pool.

Some of my friends, now well into middle age, are afraid of crabs. They may look threatening at times, but there is no point in wasting time on being dainty. Attack is the best form of defence against crabs, velvets in particular. The way I catch a crab is by stabbing at its back with my fingers, trapping it firmly against the sea bed. I then shuffle it around so that I can put a finger and thumb overlapping each side of the shell. As I lift the crab, the tip of the finger and thumb press against the sockets of the claws, rendering the crab helpless. Using the same grip, I then hold the crab firmly against the thigh of my wader while I test it. Non-peeler edibles usually grab hold of the rubber and can give the unwary a pinch if they take in a fold of skin, too. I leave them to swing there while I continue crabbing; they fall off soon enough.

Other species of crab make useful baits. Large hermit crabs, which live in whelk shells, are handy for surf fishing. Sometimes scallop dredgers bring them ashore, and sometimes they get washed in by rough seas. They can be evicted from their shells either by shaking them out or by heating the tip of the shell with a lighter. One August, years ago, a commercial fisherman found his trammel nets stuffed full of spider crabs, many of them peelers. My friend and I took a fish box full up to Beachy Head Ledge. They smelt somewhat strong, and I do not think the bass were too keen on them because we only caught two fish.

Storage and Preparation

Dead crabs go bad very rapidly, so hard-won peelers and softies need to be taken care of quickly if they are not for immediate use. This happens even when the crab is still alive and looking healthy, so I do not try to keep edibles and velvet swimmers alive. Shore crabs are more adaptable and can be kept alive for a long time with a daily drink of sea water. They can be stored in wide plastic boxes with some wet gravel to bury into and some weed to hide under. Do not put them into a tank of festering sea water or they will die. Fresh water is anathema, and no bait should be allowed to be saturated with rain water. Help the crabs to settle down by keeping them in darkness. Cover the tank with a piece of old carpet and keep them cool on the garage floor. Whatever container is used, tall sides prevent escape.

Edibles can be kept alive in a tank containing a little sea water. It is best to use underbed filters connected to a pump. A couple of

BAITS

small airstones connected to another pump will keep the crabs content. Inspect them regularly, so they do not peel and become soft and watery or worse, tinny. As soon as the tell-tale crack shows, whip them out and prepare them for the freezer.

Moulting can be slowed down by chilling the crabs in a saltwater aquarium with a few inches of water in the bottom. The water is pumped through a beer cooler to keep the temperature around 5°C (41°F). This enables you to take home crabs that are not quite ready to peel and bring them on. As they reach the peeling stage, they are either used immediately or frozen down.

To prepare a crab for bait, first crack the seam around the back where the top shell joins the lower one. Now remove the top shell. If it is too thick and risks tearing the bait, crack it by tapping it with the back of a knife. Now pick off as much as possible of the lower shell, including the apron. Whiffler peelers have such thin, friable shells that the undershell comes away by rolling the crab between your hands. The shells of edible crabs are much thicker and they make useful baits even when the toenail is not perfectly formed and the soft new shell is still a bit thin. Big, crisp edibles can be peeled again, revealing a new skin forming underneath, although they do not last long as baits. This does not work with shore crabs or velvet swimmers. The toenail must be fully formed or the ensuing bait will fall to pieces during preparation. I am also convinced that the closer a crab is to peeling, the better bait it makes. I prefer my peelers to have a wide crack around the back of the shell. Indeed, one of the easy ways of testing a peeler is to squeeze the seam where the top shell joins the lower shell. With peelers it cracks easily.

Friends of mine once met an angler who was fishing with a hard edible crab that he had just converted into a peeler, although it was nothing of the sort. He snagged up and lost his bait. My friend caught a six-pounder a little later. When he gutted it, it was found to contain the converted hard back.

I prefer a good-sized bait (at least the size of a matchbox), and I tie small crabs to my hook in bundles of two or three. I cut larger crabs in half, and mount both halves onto the hook. This allows the juices to flow and makes the bait more attractive. I always remove the legs and claws of large edible and whiffler crabs. Whenever possible, I peel them, lay them side by side, and bundle them together with elastic thread (shirring elastic). Bundles of peeled legs and claws make extremely attractive baits. With smaller crabs, I leave the legs on one side and mount the crab so that its legs point up the line. This compels the bass to take the bait from the easy side, which is where the hook is.

In hot weather, freeze crabs promptly before any off-flavours have had a chance to develop. Alternatively, shade and a block of ice will keep them fresh. An easy way to make blocks of ice is to fill plastic drinking bottles with water and freeze them. As the ice melts, the bottle retains the water and prevents it from making a mess. A cool-bag (boxes are more bulky) is a useful asset under these circumstances, and you can put a block of ice inside it.

For short-term use, crabs are easily frozen in clean, airtight plastic boxes, like those for ice-cream and margarine. Small crabs are frozen whole. Large crabs are more bulky and should be killed by stabbing the point of a knife straight through the middle from underneath. The legs and claws are then removed but not the shell before they are packed into boxes for freezing. Big crabs peel more easily after freezing.

For long-term freezing, the gills must be removed or they will fester, even when frozen. Peel the crab, then fold back the body flaps and snip away the gills with scissors. They can be individually wrapped in cling film. Rapid freezing is best, and the way to do this is to keep a metal tray in the freezer, so that the crabs are laid out on a freezing surface. The faster they freeze, the longer they last.

It is important to lock the bait onto the hook. Some anglers use treble hooks for this, but I prefer the Mustad 79510, size 4/0. It has a turned-down eye, which stops the turns of thread from rolling onto the trace. Lay the hook across the bait, towards the back of its belly, with the point protruding clear. Take 1ft (0.3m) or so of elastic thread and roughly wrap the hook onto the bait. Now take a turn of thread just below the hook's eye, take the thread under the bait (i.e. across its back), and take another turn around the hook bend. Keeping the thread tight, repeat this four more times. To lock the hook in place, hold it by the eye and take several figure-of-eight turns between the eye and the bend along the crab's belly, snap off the loose end, and secure it with a couple of half-hitches.

The bait is now firmly locked onto the hook and can be cast some distance without slipping and masking the point. Incidentally, this is a very good reason for removing the crab's claws. I have had them jam inside the bend of the hook and have lost the fish. If a small crab is used, and there is no need to cast far, the hook can be slipped through the socket of one claw and out of another.

The bait is now firmly locked onto the hook and makes a good foundation for the next bait. I often tie another crab on top of the old one when the bait needs freshening up, but once the turns of thread start balling up, I cut them off and start again. Bass thrash their heads from side to side when hooked, which often sends the bait sliding up the trace. On one occasion I caught three seven-pounders in rapid succession from the same spot – the intersection of two narrow gullies. All I did was slide the bait back onto the hook,

squeeze it and cast out again. Be gentle when casting crabs so that they stay properly mounted and do not choke the hook. Another refinement is to stab the bait with the point of a knife, or give it a good squeeze, to release juices and make it more attractive. Sometimes, I thread a peeled claw onto the bend of the hook for extra flavour.

I have used live peelers by wrapping an elastic band around them and then looping the hook around the band so that the crab can swim upright. The band should not be tight or the crab will suffocate. Eric Mesmer taught me this trick; he used it successfully to catch bass on hard backs.

Elastic thread is essential for mounting crabs and other baits, and thicker, stronger thread is best. The wise angler buys several spools to avoid running out when the bass are feeding but the shops are shut. Take care of the spool of thread or it will tangle and become hard to use – and do not mislay it!

It is usually worth preparing several baits at home, tying them onto short traces that end with a large loop. Each bait is then wrapped in cling-film and popped into a polythene bag. Freeze them, or keep them in the fridge until they are required for use. To rebait, unloop one trace and loop on the next one. It really is that simple. This rapid turn around allows two or three fish to be taken from a shoal before it moves on. It is a good idea to tie up some baits so that they can be mounted on hair rigs. Anchor a short length of soft, fine line inside the bait, at the most aerodynamic end. If you tie an open slip-knot at the other end, the bait can be quickly be attached to the hook.

Nowadays I always use groundbait when fishing with crab. I have made a giant nutcracker to crush hard backs. Every ten minutes I throw some crushed crab into the swim or use a coarse angler's magapult when fishing further out.

BAITS

PRAWNS AND SHRIMPS

Prawns are an effective bait and can be readily caught with a spoon net from pools in weedy gullies. They can also be caught at night by shining a torch into the rock pools. Their eyes show up as tiny scarlet jewels, and it is no trouble to scoop them out with a small net – like the ones sold by aquarists. They can also be caught from the weed around pier piles, and they like living in old car tyres that are used as fenders along docksides. Bunters, which are prawns in brackish water, can often be caught in large numbers, but I find it easier to lamp them when they come to the edges of their pools at night.

From a boat, the large prawn (*Leander serratus*) can be caught in baited pots, similar to those used for crabs but with finer meshes and cut-down plastic funnels for openings. However, the law requires these to be inspected every hour. Prawns are hooked from the belly outwards at the bend of the tail, using a size 2 short-shank carp hook. Large prawns are fished singly, small ones and bunters in bunches. A bunch of prawns has a lot of movement, which is what bass are looking for. Dead prawns are completely useless. Cooked ones are even worse, although ½lb (230g) of them on a large hook might interest a lunker in the autumn.

Small bass eat a lot of shrimps, but these are rarely effective as bait. The fat females move into the more sheltered sandy shallows in January, when laden with eggs. They can easily be caught in a push net at low tide, and should be fished in bunches if you wish to pursue early-season schoolies in the West Country. I occasionally hook shrimps while reeling in a sharp hook on Atlantic surf beaches. A big bunch might make a good bait.

None of these species was designed to move fast, although the speed with which a big *Leander* can bolt away is impressive, but

Prawning: at least you can eat the bait if the bass don't.

that is in calm water. Prawns work best as bait on big spring tides and in clear water surfs when the sea drags them from their hideyholes. They are very effective at night, when they come out to feed, and most of the bass that are caught on them are hooked close to walls, steep rock faces and pier piles. This is one bait that should always be plopped at the edge, on skinny float tackle, if the snags allow.

Prawns and shrimps live for a long time in wet bladderwrack. As lively (as opposed to alive) prawns catch most fish, they need to be kept in a box with a firm lid with holes punched in it, or in a small knitted-mesh keep net with the end tied shut, suspended in the sea. They seem to live forever in an aquarium, spending their days rolling over the topmost pieces of gravel and cleaning them of algae. When they moult, their cast-off shell is amazingly beautiful.

BAITS

Large prawns are deadly when fished alive under a float.

FISH BAITS

Bass spend most of their time catching and eating small fish, particularly offshore. Mackerel is one of the most effective baits for bass, both alive and dead. It is as useful as peeler crabs and much more easy to catch and use. When I first started using livebaits offshore, mackerel were sometimes hard to catch. It was often a case of catch a mackerel, catch a bass, so I had to find a way of ensuring that every mackerel that saw my string of feathers would attack them and get hooked.

Mackerel can be tricky to catch at times, particularly when feeding on plankton. They swim along slowly and strain these micro-organisms through the bristles in their gill rakers. Fortunately they spend much more time attacking fry. They are built for speed; when a mackerel sees something that looks like a small fish it hurls itself at it. If it doesn't pin it first time, it rarely comes back for a second go. Consequently, I often used to feel a tap on my feathers, then nothing. I decided to make them more attractive and increase my chances of catching them for bait.

Herring are excellent baits, alive or dead.

BAITS

The colour red appeals to predators, probably because it looks like blood. It changes 15ft (4.5m) down, so the fish must see it differently and nobody really knows precisely what wavelengths of light the fish tune in to. Anyway, it looks red to us and suggests that the prey is injured. Silver is the colour of small fry. I have always made my own feathers, and I tied some up on small stainless-steel hooks, so that rust would not discolour the dressing.

This is how to do it. Fix a size 4 or 6 hook into the vice and take twenty touching turns of fine nylon thread back from the eye. Take a small tuft of silver Lureflash, mix it with a quarter as much red Lureflash, and tie it in. In the absence of this material, a teased out strip of white polypropylene parcel string should suffice, and a tiny tuft of red wool. Cut off the end of the Lureflash, apply some polyurethane varnish, and build up the head. Whip-finish, apply a bit more varnish, then allow the 'feather' to dry. After a couple of days, paint the head white and let it dry again. As a finishing touch, paint a black dot on each side of the head, like eyes. The most obvious part of fry is their eyes, which is probably why these feathers continue to be effective long after most of the tinsel has been stripped away through hard use. Indeed, a string of stainless hooks is often as effective when the fish are striking small fry in clear water.

To string these feathers together, cut some 30lb (13.6kg) nylon into seven 18in (45cm) lengths. These are blood-knotted together, leaving one long loose end at each connection. The feathers are knotted to these. A swivel is then tied to one end, a lead clip to the other, and all the loose ends are trimmed back. Despite all the knots, this string is good for several hundred fish. Last year I used one string all season. The only time the knots pop is when pulling out of a snag.

The best way to store feathers is to wind them around a block of polythene foam. Cut a shallow 'V' at each end, and a slot to one side. Put the swivel end into the slot, wind the line around the foam and push the hook points into it. The lead clip also fits into a slot. Make three or four sets to replace those that are lost to snags. They can be cast out from the shore, but heavier nylon is required and fewer feathers,

Like bass, mackerel have several regular ambush points where they can herd up the baitfish and set about them, but you are likely to find them anywhere that the water is clear. They dislike cloudy seas and swarm where they can see for miles. From the shore, they are often found chasing baitfish into the beach around jetties and piers, in the ebb currents from estuaries, around rocky headlands, and other places that focus the fry. Look out for skipping baitfish, followed by splashy swirls or a frenzied foaming on the surface as they drive into the fry, their mouths open, straining small fish through their gill rakers.

When fishing from a boat, mackerel may be at any depth, so the entire water column may need to be explored. Usually, joey mackerel are within 10–20ft (3–6m) of the surface, sometimes 30ft (9m). Hunting gannets are a useful clue: if they are up aloft looking for prey, the baitfish are not deep.

The easiest way to mount a dead fish bait is to put the hook up through the lips.

A plentiful supply of mackerel is necessary when using them for groundbait.

Mackerel shoals can often be seen on the surface or on the screen of the fish finder, but sometimes they are much more elusive. It should be remembered that mackerel eat a lot of oily fish and what goes in ultimately goes out, leaving an oil slick on the surface that can sometimes be seen a mile away. Most conveniently, mackerel often hover high above the same wrecks and reefs that attract bass.

At the stern of my boat are two rod rests, angled outwards for trolling and mackerel fishing. The feathers are set to fish at a certain depth, and the rods are put into the rests. The feathers are worked by the boat rolling with the waves. This is a handy trick when mackerel are scarce and you are tired of holding the rod and flicking the feathers up and down. It is almost as effective as doing it properly, but not quite. It reveals the presence of a shoal, but does not catch the odd lone fish so well.

From the boat, it is worthwhile fishing a small pirk at the bottom of the feathers to con the mackerel into thinking that another fish is attacking baitfish. Usually, though, an 8oz (227g) lead weight is sufficient. Quite a heavy lead is needed or the mackerel will tangle the feathers into a ball – another good reason for carrying spares.

When the first mackerel is hooked, start reeling slowly to keep everything under control. More fish are likely to attack the feathers, maybe a full house, one on each hook. Reel in, reach over the side of the boat, grab the lower end of the trace, and lift them aboard. Some anglers can unhook them by holding the weight and flicking the rod, but I can't. I unhook them by holding the head of the feather and letting the mackerel shake itself free. Any that are not bleeding can be unhooked directly into the livebait tank. (A fish that is bleeding will pollute the tank in seconds, and unless the water is cleared, the others may die.) Otherwise, tap the mackerel on its head and put it in a bucket. The best bucket is a tall, narrow one. It prevents the fish from flapping around and splashing blood and scales everywhere.

These home-made feathers are highly effective against many species of fish that feed on fry: herring, scad (horse mackerel), small pouting, whiting, greater launce, and sometimes garfish. Schoolies throw themselves at them with gay abandon, which is irritating as each fish has to be carefully unhooked and dropped back overboard.

Chunks of garfish make useful baits, but these fish are most easily caught on light float tackle baited with a slender strip of mackerel skin. So are smelt, in harbours, using very small hooks and matching baits. Some anglers have caught bass on chunks of silver eel, which can readily be taken from estuaries and marshland dykes on bits of fish or crab. Some people use little bootlace eels as bait, but I consider them disgusting ill-mannered creatures and have nothing to do with them.

The point about any bass bait is that it has to have maximum appeal to the fish, so each fish that gets frozen down needs to be properly prepared. Small herrings, wrasse and joey mackerel are best frozen whole, but many others would be effective if a bass came across them. Frozen imported sardines are also effective. If you can obtain a short length of 10mm (inside diameter) stainless steel tube, sharpen one end and use it to remove the back bone. This makes the bait more supple and succulent, and you do not have to slice and, therefore, weaken it. Insert the sharpened tube into the gills, cut through the back bone at an angle, and slide the tube over the bone to the tail before snapping it off. The back bone is then removed and shaken out of the tube. Wrap each fish tightly in cling-film to keep out the oxygen, which makes fats rancid.

Deadbaits are always swallowed head first. You can thread the hook under the skin from the tail, and tie the trace around the waist with elastic thread. A 4/0 – 6/0 hook protrudes from the gill-cover. For short-range work or boat fishing it is easiest to hook it through both lips, with the point emerging from the top of the head.

The head and guts of small mackerel make good baits but I am not so sure about the head of large mackerel. On may occasions I have caught bass of 6–10lbs, which have taken a dead mackerel and swallowed it straight down. Most times when a bass finds a large head it plays around with it. There is a lot of knocking on the rod-tip, sometimes a proper run, then nothing. It seems as if the fish is not sure what angle to swallow the bait at. The head lacks the streamline effect of the body, so the package cannot easily be turned round and swallowed. Large mackerel heads attract plenty of offers, but they do not convert into as many hooked fish as a long slim slice. Perhaps I should fish them on a hair rig.

Eric Mesmer often told me that a fish bait was much more effective with eyes, but I have found bass to be much easier to hook when baiting with a strip of mackerel. The way I do it now is to split the head in half and fillet the mackerel, discarding the back bone and tail. This leaves a large area from where the natural juices can seep out, and the light colour stands out better on a rocky or weedy sea-bed. Mackerel is most effective in clear water, and as bass spend the greater part of each day hunting by sight, a light-coloured bait is easier for them to track down.

When I hook on a slim slice of fish, I prefer to have the hook protruding from the skin side. Often I use the long stub of a knot, pointing back up the line, as a bait holder. A thin strip is hooked once through one end, but a thicker slice is hooked twice, using the stub to restrain the bait when I lob it into the

Mackerel are the most enjoyable bait to catch.

BAITS

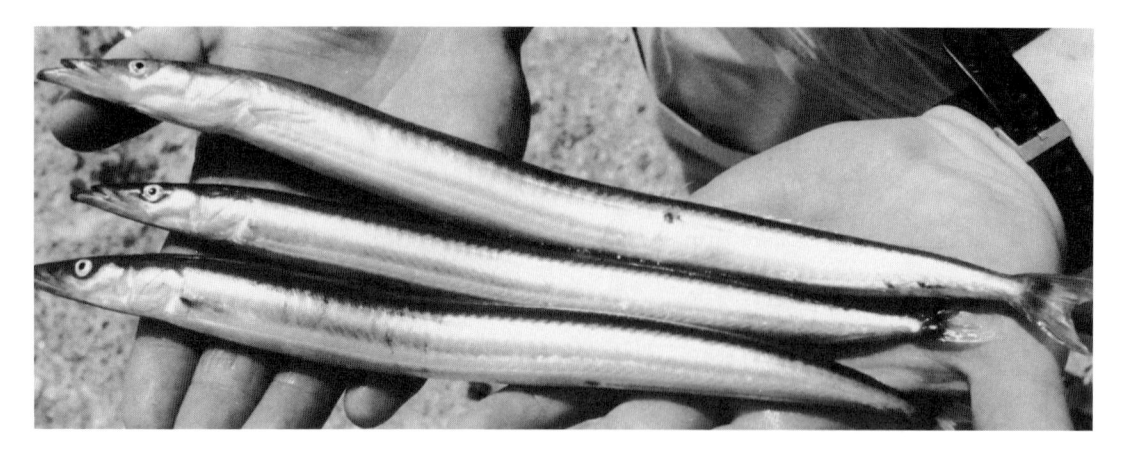

Launce, like all sandeels, are a deadly bait.

swim. If you have to fish with a slice of stale or frozen mackerel, hook it from the thick end, or the tide runs against the grain of the flesh and turns it into a ragged mess.

Around piers and reefs, pouting, poor cod and wrasse can be taken close to the bottom on a three-hook paternoster, fishing with bits of lugworm or crab on tiny hooks. Bass love them, but – like whiting – they are hard to keep alive if they are taken from deep water. The swim bladder blows up. Whitebait can sometimes be caught near piers, rocks, and open beaches with a cast net, and so can mackerel as I discovered last autumn when they were striking whitebait: I got twelve in one cast.

Bass love eating sandeels, and they are a phenomenal bait that can be caught with a 'vingler' (a blade with a hook at the end). This is worked in a figure-of-eight through wet sand along the tide line, and any resistance usually signifies a sandeel, which is raised to the surface and captured before it can skitter away. They can also be evicted by stomping along the surf line in your

A floating wooden courge is ideal for keeping sandeels alive.

BAITS

waders, using the aquarium net to catch them. A 50yd (46m) seine net catches many more, using a boat to encircle the shoals. In some places, a licence is required before doing this, and it is illegal to use a seine net in a protected bass nursery area. Sandeels often swarm from the sea-bed to mid-water, particularly in sheltered sun-warmed bays. One man stands on the beach, the other goes around in a boat paying out the net, then both drag it ashore. A small aquarium net is used to transfer the catch to a big bucket of sea water without damaging them.

Sandeels are perfect for fishing wherever bass are found, but particularly in clear water. To keep them alive, insert a small carp hook through the mouth, out of the gills, and nick it in the belly. They can be used with nearly every style of fishing. Dead ones work well, particularly at night. As with all deadbaits, it pays to make them bleed a bit, and a thick needle is useful to puncture the body cavity, when used whole. A filleted launce makes an excellent bait, particularly if a few have been finely sliced and cast upon the waters. Some people trawl for big launce, others use tiny feathers off the pierhead. Live sandeels can be bought from some tackle shops, particularly in the West Country.

SQUID AND CUTTLE

Squid makes a very good bait, especially in the autumn when lots of them are around offshore. I prefer them 6in (15cm) long and very fresh. It is best to buy them straight from the trawlers or fish merchants and freeze them, or buy a box of small squid from a freezer centre or trusted

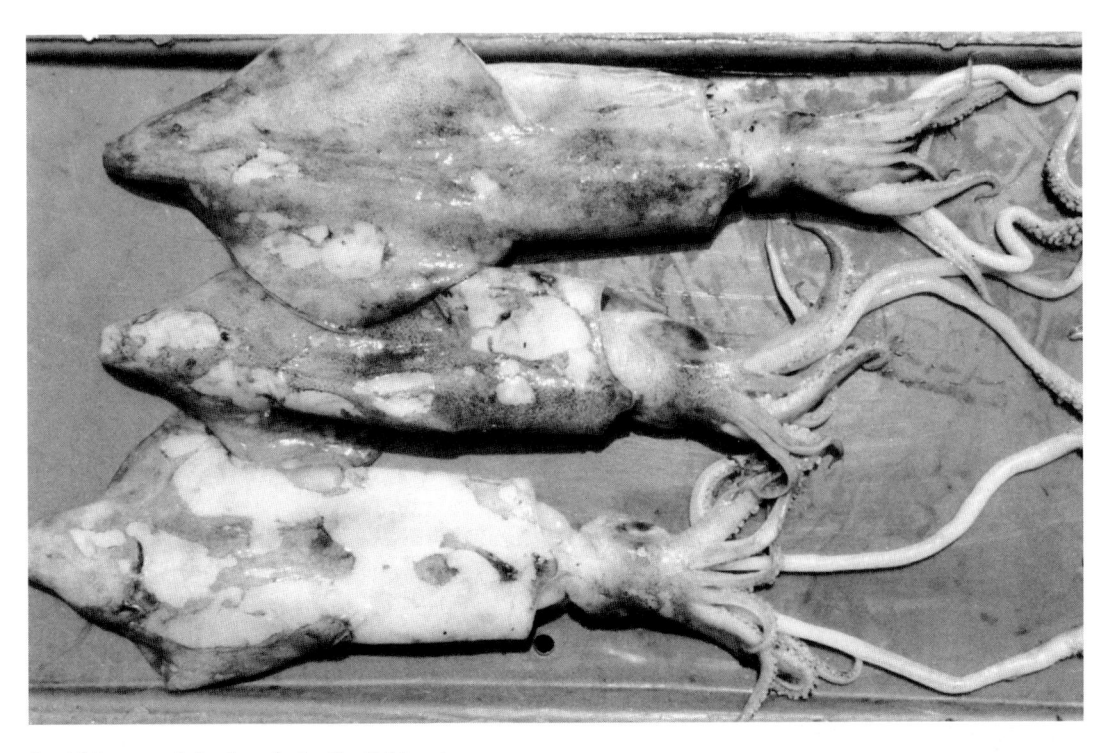

Squid is one of the best baits for fishing in autumn.

BAITS

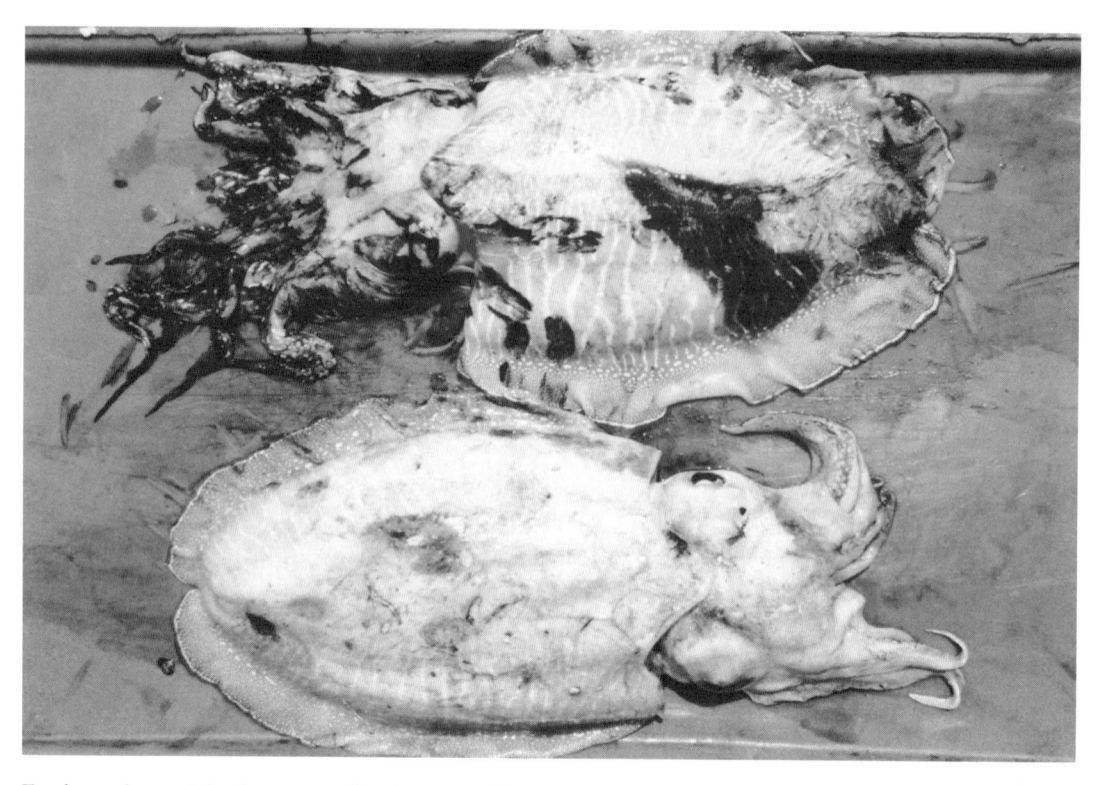

Fresh cuttle, straight from a trawler, is most effective early and late in the season.

tackle dealer. Anglers persist in calling small squid 'calamari' which is Italian for squid of any size. Even when used whole, they are best skinned, then stabbed with the knife-point to make the juices flow. Large squid can be sliced into thin strips, then tied into bundles 4–6 in (10–15cm) long. Small squid can be converted into 'lugworm squiddies' by packing them with worms and sealing them with elastic thread before perforating them with a knife. When casting these big baits, you need to thumb gently the multiplier's spool during the cast, or an over run will be inevitable.

Large squid make very good sandeel imitations when sliced very thinly. Open up the mantle, then cut full-length slices ½–1in (1–2cm) wide. If the squid is big, the thickness of the mantle could be the width of the bait. If the squid is required to move and flutter in the tide, it is best to pare away some of the thickness.

Squid is notorious for masking the hook and allowing fish to escape. Use a large hook, like a 6/0 Mustad 79515, and instead of tying the hook with a fixed knot, tie a loop. Thread it through the eye of the hook and back round on itself. Insert the hook through the squid from the pointed end. Some anglers twist the hook point outwards slightly to help it bite into the fish better. After baiting up, loosen the loop and poke ½in (1cm) of matchstick through it before tightening it again. This prevents the bait sliding down the hook and keeps the point ready for action. The same trick can be used when mounting a side of mackerel from the tail end.

I once found a lost octopus in the surf in Wales. Bass eat them when they can, but cuttlefish are highly effective for big bass. Cuttle can often be found washed up along the shore line or drifting out at sea in June and July. They die after spawning, and the gulls usually get them first, which is why only the white bones are washed in. Dead ones are best left where they lie if they stink, as they have a particularly vicious aroma. Offshore, they sometimes catch and kill mackerel livebaits. I have frequently caught cuttlefish on live mackerel while slowly drifting over wrecks. Live ones should be bounced around in a landing net until they have vented their ink. They can then be treated like large squid. Incidentally, cuttle guts are a magic bait for conger and large cod, but without the ink. These baits are more succulent and appealing if they are free of any trace of ink.

WORMS

Bass of all sizes can be caught on lugworm, especially in thick, cloudy water when the fish are scenting out their food. In autumn, big fish frequently take parcels of lug that are intended for cod. The only time lug are useful in clear water is when fishing Atlantic storm beaches. Even then I prefer a fat, white razor fish or clam. It shows up better.

The smaller types of lugworm can be trenched with a potato fork. The bigger, black lug are best dug with a proper lugworm spade or sucked out of the sand with a worm-pump, carefully following the worm's hole back to its lair. Bass hardly ever take a stale lug, and they are not too keen on worms that have dried out in newspaper or have been lounging around in a bait tank. They prefer freshly dug worms.

Packets of black lugworm – a bait with limited appeal for bass.

BAITS

King ragworm is an excellent bait but hard to get hold of.

As every mullet angler knows, baby bass are suckers for bunches of the small ragworm that are dug out of the muddy banks of estuaries. In some places it is now illegal to dig for bait, especially around nature reserves and sites of special scientific interest. Check on this before plunging your fork into hallowed ground. Bass often encounter ragworms in the spring, when they come out of their holes and form large spawning congregations.

King ragworm is a very effective bait when fished on a long trace over shallow offshore sandbanks and in the surf, but watch out for their fangs. Lively, wriggling ragworms are among the best baits for float fishing. White ragworms can be dug for in many areas of muddy sand, and are a handy bait. All worms can be stored in the cool in dry newspaper, if regularly changed, but white rags need to be kept in sand with a few inches of clean sea water over it.

Some of the best ragworms are a 1yd (0.9m) long and as thick as your thumb. Cutlets of them make excellent baits in the surf, although in places like Anglesey, huge boulders have to be shifted along the low water mark on big tides before digging can begin in the sloppy mud. The best sites for ragworm are generally a closely guarded secret. Nowadays they are farmed, which makes life easier. They are much more successful than lugworm after being kept in an aerated aquarium.

White ragworm is usually more trouble than it is worth for bass fishing.

BAITS

RAZOR FISH, CLAMS AND SHELLFISH

Razor fish are an excellent bait, and so too are clams. Razors can be located in their holes by squirts of water out of the sand, or a slight upwelling of wet sand as they escape by digging. They can be dug out of their beds, evicted by pouring cooking salt down their oval holes, or speared with a length of thick wire with a barb each side of the point. Spear the razor fish, turn the spear through one right angle, and gently withdraw the bait. Razor fish are sometimes washed ashore in large numbers after winter storms and can be frozen down whole.

Clams are found in sheltered areas of muddy sand and have to be dug out with a fork. Fortunately they can not move through sand as fast as razor fish. It is best to pile as much of the clam or razor fish onto the 4/0 hook as possible, threading it from the tip of the syphon. A clam's syphon looks better if it

Most types of shellfish make effective baits.

Razor-fish make tough, juicy baits for surf fishing.

BAITS

Digging bait: strenuous preparation for a day's fishing.

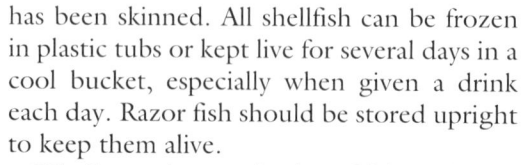

Clams are tough and make sturdy eye-catching baits for the surf.

has been skinned. All shellfish can be frozen in plastic tubs or kept live for several days in a cool bucket, especially when given a drink each day. Razor fish should be stored upright to keep them alive.

Whelks used to catch a lot of fish in the old days. They are readily caught in specially designed pots, but it is many years since I heard of anybody baiting up with them for bass. Slipper limpets can be very good for general beach fishing, especially after storms. They live in clusters, which get smashed apart by rough seas. Otherwise, the bass would never find them. Using a blunt knife, separate the slipper limpets and shell them onto a wad of newspaper to dry a little. Thread them up the hook shank and onto a line, then put a strip of squid on each side of the bundle, like splints. Tie them in place with elastic thread, and then tie the package to a 4/0 hook – Mustad 79515.

OTHER BAITS

Bass are opportunist feeders and gorge themselves when they find an abundant supply of food. They sometimes become preoccupied with slaters, sandhoppers, and seaweed maggots when these get caught out by big tides or rough seas. Bass have been taken on all sorts of baits, and kipper is still one of the favourite autumn baits around here. Smoked salmon skins work equally well. As always, if an opportunity presents itself for catching bass, make the most of it.

Whatever bait is used, keep it out of reach of foxes, which often patrol the shore line; rats too. I was once fishing, reclined on the shingle, and a party of fox cubs came padding along the shingle within a few feet of me. Once, when camping at Dungeness, they got into the tent and stole all our food. They even licked out the lugworm bucket.

104

6 Boating for Bass

When you head offshore, your safety – and that of the crew – depends entirely on how fit the boat is for the open sea. Weather conditions can change rapidly out there, and as bass often feed well in rough weather, it is not uncommon for bass boats to get caught out in nasty seas. You must be confident that the boat will withstand these conditions and will bring you back safely to harbour. There are no places to pull in out there, so a well-designed, properly maintained boat is essential.

The phrase 'Oh, we'll be all right' has no place at sea as I discovered in May 1984 when a friend and I rode forth to tackle vast shoals of bass that had assembled off Beachy Head. The engine was coughing on the way up there. I caught a 26lb cod on the first drift, then the engine refused to start. It had blown its main bearing. We dropped the anchor, but it was six hours before a trawler noticed our distress signals in a rising gale and notified the lifeboat. The crew rescued two very sheepish, exhausted anglers.

We should have known better, and we were lucky. That lesson taught me deep respect for the sea. Lifeboatmen have no gripes about rescuing anglers who, despite all their efforts and a carefully maintained boat, fall foul of the sea – it happens – but 90 per cent of breakdowns could have been avoided by simple maintenance or an extra can of fuel. Bass anglers travel far and expose themselves to many dangers, so join the RNLI. Take out a generous covenant and support them at every opportunity. The 50p you donated last time a collecting box was shaken under your nose looks woefully inadequate when a million pound boat plucks you from a watery grave.

Trawler skippers have no manners whatsoever. They are out to scoop up what they can,

This boat is a disaster looking for somewhere to happen.

BOATING FOR BASS

and sometimes seem prepared to sink anybody who gets in their way. Out of Newhaven, they often attack bass boats, even though they were onto the shoal long before the trawlermen were out of bed. Once, out on my own and miles from land, I had to hustle a nine-and-a-half pounder into the net because a trawlerman realized that I had pinpointed a tiny wreck that is hard to find. I hooked the fish on my first drift, but I had to watch the trawler bearing down on me. I had just enough time to net the fish, start the engine, and spin the boat out of his way. He missed me by about 6ft (2m), then set trammel nets all around the wreck. I had to fish somewhere else.

Sunday charter skippers are little better when they are desperate to find their crew some fish, which is why I rarely go out on a Sunday. When the sea is flat and the sun is bright, charter boats, diving boats, fishing club boats and everybody else want to have certain wrecks to themselves. The arguments that break out over the radio are quite hilarious. The rule should be first-come, first-served, unless the other boat invites you to join in.

The sea is such a corrosive environment that boats require constant maintenance, yet on the first sunny weekend each summer, you can see derelict jalopies pop-popping out to sea with engines that have not been serviced since the previous year. Anybody who does not take pride in his boat is asking for trouble. During the rough-and-tumble of a busy fishing season, something always needs fixing or maintaining. These problems have to be dealt with before they get worse.

Most bass boats are 14–22ft (4–7m) long, but smaller boats are best for working close to shore. Small boats do not disturb bass as much as big ones. There are three main designs of hull: displacement, cathedral and deep vee. Displacement hulls are slow because they push through the water, but they ride the sea well especially at anchor, and are handy for fishing inshore. The cathedral hull, like the deep vee, is designed to plane over the sea. The gull-wing shape of a cathedral hull makes it very stable – like my first boat, a 14ft (4m) dory. However, the blunt nose of a dory slams in choppy seas, which is why my current boat is a deep vee. It slices through the waves better, although it is not quite as stable. Some modern hulls combine the best of the dory and deep vee designs.

My boat is built to withstand hard use. The bottom is a sandwich of glass fibre with blocks of balsawood in the middle. It is 1½in (4cm) thick and very strong. My chum, who had the boat before me, customized it and did a lot of work on it. I, too, have done a lot of work on it, so I know every inch of the hull, the strength of the fabric, and every bolt and fitting. This enables me to detect any problems before they get serious. Likewise the engine: its note is firmly engrained in my head, and I can locate a problem before it develops. The engine needs to be powerful enough for the boat. Most anglers use outboards, which are very reliable. My Mariner 55 has never let me down in ten years of service. Regular maintenance is essential, so it helps if your circle of friends includes at least one first-class mechanic.

There are many variations in hull and engine design, and you have to take account of whether the boat will be launched from the beach or a trailer, or if it will be kept at a permanent mooring. Unfortunately, space decrees that all of this lies outside the scope of this chapter, which is about how to equip and run a bass boat, but I will make one point. I sometimes take my boat into very shallow, rocky places. A steel keel band and wooden bilge keels prevent damage to the hull in these tight corners. They are also essential protection for the hull when launching off the beach.

I have fond memories of beach launching in my dory, getting everything ship-shape before

BOATING FOR BASS

Those were the days: winching my dory up onto the promenade.

that heave through the surf and the powerful sweep on the oars to reach the more gentle water farther out, then the magic moment when the outboard started first time, having been primed on the beach. I did it for years, and luckily for me the sea was always forgiving of my occasional foolishness.

It is great fun to come in at speed and slither gracefully up the shingle rather than to land with a crash in the surf, having run out of petrol. I made two large bung holes for rapid draining on my dory because you can do a lot of damage by flying ashore off the top of a wave, and I preferred to land just beyond the surf. Sometimes I got it wrong, the boat got swamped, and we had to swim out to retrieve the bass and tackle boxes as they floated away on the waves.

In rough weather, the boat had to be winched 10ft (3m) up off the beach. When it was launched again, it was tipped over the edge and slid down a giant ladder made from old roof timbers, arriving on the beach with a head-turning crash. Those were the days. Heaving boats around keeps you fit, especially when your energies are fuelled by the prospect of a decent catch. Nowadays, I rent a hole in the water in the harbour, and have quite enough aerobics offshore.

FUEL

Everything to do with fuel needs to be kept clean to prevent dirt blocking up jets and valves. Modern engines have oil injection. It is another thing that can fail, and every so often it does. That is why I like to mix the oil with the petrol before going afloat. My engine runs on a 50:1 petrol/oil mix, and I buy top-quality outboard oil (cheap stuff fouls up spark plugs) in 40l drums. I pour it into a container with a small tap at the bottom. It is measured out in a jug (13fl oz per jerry can). A rag is draped over the jug to keep out grit and moths, which tend to fall into it and die at the bottom.

The main fuel tank, which is plastic to avoid corrosion, is refuelled by jerry cans. After each trip, to avoid the risk of using petrol that has not had oil added to it, I always put the oil in before the cans are put back in the garage. Fail-safe routines like this are essential, or you may become a victim of Murphy's Law. Jerry cans are a convenient way of refuelling, but they are not salt water proof. I buy mine second-hand from an army surplus store. I do not trust the caps on plastic ones, and some flimsy ones that are currently on the market will block the carburettor with tiny flakes of

BOATING FOR BASS

Carry plenty of fuel, and store it securely.

paint. They are not as good as the old army ones. Two of mine are dated 1945 – a few months older than I am.

It is best to paint metal jerry cans before subjecting them to saltwater spray. They are easy to rub down, degrease, and paint with a primer, followed by a couple of coats of tough one-shot gloss paint. Red is the recognized colour for petrol cans. I poke wire through the hinge and hang them on the washing line before painting the bottom. When the paint is dry, I grease the hinge of the lid. If the rubber seal is old and leaky, I pick it out with the point of a knife and put it back the other way.

To avoid spilling petrol while refuelling, I use a large rectangular funnel with a gauze filter and fluting down the outside to let the air escape from the tank. Otherwise, it would bubble over and spill. A round funnel is inferior because the movement of the boat will cause a wave of fuel to slop around, and spillages are inevitable. While refuelling, I brace myself against the side of the boat and support the can and my arms against my knees while pouring. This is always done with the lid of the can uppermost.

Fast boats bounce like crazy, so absolutely everything needs to be tied down and secured, especially the jerrycans. I have stuck wooden blocks to the side of the hull for this purpose. Two holes were drilled through each block to take lengths of rope for tying the cans in place. The blocks were fixed to the glass fibre by removing the paint from areas the same size as each block, roughing up the glass and each block with the end of a file, then sticking each in place with Sikaflex 221. A strip of tape holds the blocks in place while the mastic is curing. Strapped in like this, the

The lid of a jerrycan, greased to prevent rust and fuel leaks.

BOATING FOR BASS

Sikaflex is the best mastic for boat building, but silicon rubber is better for windows (which sometimes need to be replaced) as it is less tenacious. My boat is full of Sikaflex. I have used it to glue the floorboards in place, to attach the helm to the hull, to seal every bolt hole and washer, to glue thick marine ply to the transom before glassing it in, and for making all sorts of fastenings rather than risking the integrity of the hull by drilling holes through it.

Always take plenty of fuel in case you wish to bring home a heavy weight of fish, or you are slowed down by big seas and other situations that guzzle gas. Always check the amount of fuel in the tank before approaching harbour: It does not look very professional to run out of fuel in front of the Harbour Master's office when a ferry is bearing down on you. Always refuel when the weather turns bad and you have to dash for home. The last thing you want is to be wallowing around in rough seas with a petrol can – even worse with an empty can.

A wooden block, stuck to the hull with Sikaflex, makes a useful anchorage for items of equipment.

jerrycans can be used to trim the balance of the boat, according to the weight of the crew.

One day I was pounding back through a choppy sea and discovered the boat was awash with fuel. I had omitted to saw off the ends of the bilge keel bolts, and one had pounded through the bottom of a jerrycan. I stopped the boat, turned on the bilge pump and the one for the livebait tank, and squirted water all over the floor and scrubbed it clean. This lifted the spilt fuel and the bilge pump dumped it overboard. Next day, I cut the bolt ends flush with the nuts and covered them with Upol-B, a glass fibre jam that is very useful in boat building. All my keel bolts pass through blocks of it because the balsawood between the inner and outer skins used to allow them to shift and leak.

ELECTRONICS

Boats for inshore work require little in the way of electronics, apart from a fish finder. For fishing offshore, navigation equipment is essential, not least because landmarks are useless in hazy weather. In mist and fog, especially where high-speed ferries ply their trade, radar may be required, or at least a radar reflector.

The fish finder needs to be water-proof for use in an open boat, and several suitable machines are available. Old-fashioned models used paper traces, and everybody was assured that the paper could be saved and referred to, which is rubbish because the position of the boat has not been included. My Lowrance X60 fish finder has a liquid crystal display, and is immune to all the flying spray and pounding

109

BOATING FOR BASS

The transducer for the fish finder needs to be correctly positioned for maximum effect.

that it has to put up with. The transducer, which broadcasts and receives the electronic pulses, is mounted outside the hull, where it is marginally more sensitive than one fitted inside but is more exposed to damage. Cuts in the cable allow salt water to rot the copper wire, which ruins it. A 3-D fish finder can be used up to a certain depth, but I doubt if it enables more fish to be caught. Whatever model is chosen, it must be compact.

Basic equipment for navigating – and for spying on other bass boats.

A colour fish finder is bulky and a waste of money if you know what you are looking for. The colour option consumes a lot of battery power. Bass, like other big fish, show up as red blobs on the screen, but it is just as easy to differentiate between species by observing their position in relation to the structure. (Bass are usually up-tide of it.)

My fish finder has all sorts of useful functions, like zoom, alarms and fish symbols that distinguish between small fish and lunkers. It is very exciting, after setting out at some absurd hour of the morning, to arrive at my destination and see large fish symbols flashing up on the screen.

Electronic navigation aids, like the Decca and the Global Positioning System (GPS), are so accurate that anglers can go whizzing out to wrecks and reefs far beyond the horizon and find them easily. You just tap in the destination, watch the screen, follow the rolling road, and the navigator does the rest. The Decca system works off land-based radio beacons. It works well in the West Country, but is not very good off south-east England. Readings become unreliable at night, in thundery weather and in winter, so I have scant use for the system. GPS works off a constellation of satellites around the globe. The readings are very accurate, and are never affected by interference. GPS is an American military system. The Russians have an inferior one of their own. Some receivers can read from both systems – and Decca or Loran (the American equivalent) – at the same time, but they are bulky and guzzle electricity.

Because GPS is a military system, it offers 'variable availability', which means that civilian sets do not receive all the signals that military sets do and are therefore less accurate. The system is capable of accuracy down to 1/1000th of a minute in both latitude and longitude. That is a rectangle measuring 6ft × 4ft (2m × 1m). However, civilians have to wait for an American invasion before they get accuracy like this.

The deliberate inaccuracy which GPS Headquarters in the USA tunes into the system can be reduced by using a 'differential' receiver. The differential is the difference between the position supplied by the GPS satellites and the true position. This is broadcast from land-based transmitters. At the time of writing, the one at the Hook of Holland is powerful, and free. The ones around Britain are in code, and an annual licence of about £500 has to be paid for a decoder, thus proving to the world's shipping that the British are mean and unhelpful.

Special charts are available for use with Decca, but standard charts can be used with GPS. To increase their accuracy, take a long straight edge and a fine-tipped pen, and rule a line between each minute of a degree, forming a grid. Each minute of longitude is one nautical mile (2,027yds; 1,853m) and measures an inch on 1:75,000 charts. Thus, it becomes easy to read off a position with a ruler. On my chart, 1/10th of a minute measures 1/10th of an inch in longitude and 1/10th of an inch in latitude.

When setting up a GPS receiver, it needs to be programmed with the correct data so that it correlates with the chart. Most British charts are based on Ordnance Survey data. Do not be too hopeful of finding new 'virgin' wrecks. Most of those inside the 50m (55yd) line are already charted.

Rather than taking carefully prepared charts out to sea, have them photocopied. The charts can then be cut to size and put into a binder. The plastic leaves in my 'fishing book' hold important papers, like charts, details of marks and harbour signals, and keep them dry. An alternative, on a larger boat, is to use an electronic chart and a plotter. Incidentally, the first waypoint to enter into your GPS is the one that gets used most, particularly in an emergency – the harbour mouth.

111

BOATING FOR BASS

Fish finder, GPS navigator, and compass mounted close together for easy viewing. The compass looks drunk with all the electronics around it, but still works well enough. One day I'll move it.

Electronic navigators are amazing but are utterly useless when they develop a fault or the battery fails, so a compass should always be kept on board. There are three on my boat. The main one is mounted on the dashboard, so I can glance from it, to the fish finder and to the GPS without taking my eyes off the sea. A hand-held compass is useful for taking bearings, but the best one for this purpose is inside my binoculars. I can spot a boat on the horizon and note its bearing and approximate distance. With my GPS I find my position and then transfer the bearing onto the chart with a protractor. The chart reveals that one other boat is fishing an interesting lump of structure. A calm sea with good visibility is no place for privacy.

What happens when the navigator goes down? There is usually some warning, and your position should be noted before it dies completely. With a protractor and ruler, the correct bearing can be read off the chart for the homeward journey – allowing for the tide, of course.

When locating fishing marks, the easiest way is to take precise bearings from landmarks. A compass helps here, but the most accurate system is to line up prominent landmarks. The principles can easily be learned on land, when you are on a walk. Line up two prominent sets of landmarks, and you will find that these alignments are so precise that as soon as you move to one side, the perspective changes and they no longer match up. Offshore, the same degree of accuracy can be guaranteed by aligning prominent features like tall buildings, clumps of trees, radio masts, chimneys, churches, houses, fissures in the cliffs and so on. The easiest and quickest way to remember them is to sit above your fishing mark and either scan the shore line with a camera and a zoom lens or make detailed drawings. I prefer to use the camera because several different alignments can usually be found while studying the prints. With a cheap roll of film and one-hour processing, a set of photographs can be mounted in your fishing log book shortly after coming ashore. They will be invaluable the following season to refresh your memory of the alignments. The photos should be taken in good visibility or the landmarks will not show up clearly.

Landmarks vary in quality according to how the light is striking them. For example, the side of a building or a buttress of rock will stand out clearly when the sun hits it from one angle, but at another time of day, with the light coming from a different angle and a

BOATING FOR BASS

My thirty-year-old Microplus, newly fitted out for another season.

BOATING FOR BASS

different direction, it may be hard to pick out. Mist and haze reduce visibility and may obscure a radio mast or clump of trees on a hilltop several miles inland. Orange-tinted binoculars help to cut through the haze and can be used to magnify indistinct landmarks.

Navigators, differential receivers and VHF radios all have aerials which, in small boats, work better if they are held above the waves on a mast. This, too, needs to be tough enough to take a pounding. I designed the one on my boat, which is why it is held up by a cat's cradle of cables. The wooden top bar snapped in rough seas last season, which has compelled me to design a new one out of stainless-steel tube.

The mast is the ideal location for navigation lights and for lights to illuminate the cockpit while sorting out the boat after a late session. I never use them while fishing, but I have a feeble light above the helm for rebaiting after dark. My new mast has a light on each side to provide an all round spread. Reversing lights from a motor accessories shop are cheap and easy to install. They are made of plastic and do not corrode.

At least one powerful battery is required to run all the electrical and electronic equipment on board a modern bass boat. It has to start the engine, run the pumps, the fish finder, radio, navigator (although I prefer a separate battery for this, to eliminate interference) and the lights. Batteries should be secured inside a box so that they don't bounce around. My main one is in a dry place at the back of the boat. It is smaller than its allotted site, so I have made a reducer out of plywood to stop it from sliding around. A rubber mat protects it from pounding in short seas, and it is tied down with rope. The battery terminals are kept clean and are well greased to prevent corrosion. All the cables from the battery and from the engine (including the steering and throttle controls) are fitted inside a plastic drainpipe to keep them neat and tidy. The pipe has been neatly slotted inside the boat and is supported by straps of glass fibre (woven rovings). Nothing looks more shabby than dangling loops of cable.

SAFETY EQUIPMENT

Only a fool goes afloat without listening to a weather forecast, but forecasts are rarely reliable, and the ones on TV are sometimes contradictory. One channel says it will be fine; another channel warns of wind and rain. It is best to understand how the weather shapes up along your particular stretch of coast. In June, when the sea is still cold and the land warms up rapidly, thermal winds can develop very quickly and are likely to catch out the unwary. When the wind blows against the tide, the seas become considerably more lumpy. I dislike fishing with wind over tide.

A sighing breeze at midnight often means big seas in the morning. You should multiply the wind speed ½ mile (0.3km) inland by a factor of four to correlate it with conditions offshore. The Coastguard provides a full round-the-clock service of weather forecasts on the VHF radio. These are broadcast at regular four-hourly intervals. In the event of gales or strong winds, warnings are broadcast every two hours.

Flares are essential when going offshore, even if only a short distance. The lifeboat and the Coastguard helicopter investigate every sighting of a red parachute flare. The trouble is that somebody first has to see it, which is not always likely when you are 20 miles (32km) offshore in thick mid-summer haze. A VHF marine radio is essential. A licence is required for this and is easy to obtain after you have taken a course in the procedures for using a marine radio. Knowing precisely what to do in hairy moments can mean the difference between living and dying. Portable

114

marine radios and mobile telephones are also useful safety aids.

A set of decent tools is also essential. Things rarely go wrong when a boat is tied up in harbour. They usually fail when miles from land in borderline conditions, or when the fish are in a feeding frenzy. Spare spark plugs, a couple of screwdrivers, a roll of water-proof tape, some grease, a can of WD40 and a set of spanners have sorted out most problems that I have encountered in the last ten years. I keep them in a cheap plastic box from a hardware superstore. I bought two, in different colours. The other is my tackle box.

Most offshore bass boats are capable of 20–30 knots. Fast boats are great fun in flat seas, and steeple-chasing in a sloppy sea is highly enjoyable, but you need a strong hull that can take the pounding. I prefer to drive into a slight chop. A breeze seems to lift the hull and help it plane. In flat calms, it seems to stick to the sea, and the drive becomes very monotonous. Driving is most unpleasant in big following seas because you have to go very slowly, and steerage is partially lost. When heading into big seas, you have to attack the waves positively, putting on a burst of speed to overcome them so that they do not overwhelm the boat. It is hard to drive along big seas as you forever have to to turn into them when a wall of water looks threatening. To this end, you should always concentrate on where the waves are coming from. Seamanship is a seat-of-the-pants affair. Only experience can teach it to you. It is not something that can be learned from a book, but is best taught by terror and built on nightmares.

Unless you get a weather forecast like 'slack air over the English Channel will persist', a long-peaked hat and sunglasses are essential for keeping spray out of your eyes. If blinded by spray, you will be unable to respond to the next monster wave, which could be disastrous. Blinding reflections from bright sunshine are almost as bad. Ropes, pot lines, and even divers become hard to see against the glitter. If things start looking bad, put on the life jackets. If they look dangerous, radio the Coastguard and inform him of your position, destination and expected time of arrival in case disaster strikes. Before putting to sea, you should always tell somebody where you are going and when you will be back.

Driving in rough seas is exhausting and demands total concentration. For this reason, I do not permit any alcohol on my boat.

Pockets of netting restrain items of equipment and keep them safe when the boat is pounding through sloppy seas.

BOATING FOR BASS

There is ample time for drinking when we return to harbour. You should always be aware that trouble can strike at any time. The propeller may pick up a drifting rope or old net, which would not be easy to cut clear with a brain full of booze. Sometimes I have fished in perfect conditions far offshore, but on the way home have encountered rough seas that have been churned up by coastal weather.

Bass like rough seas. They excite them and get them feeding in situations that put their prey at a disadvantage. However, optimism and excessive enthusiasm have drowned more anglers than enough. He who fishes then runs away, lives to fish another day.

I always carry tins of baked beans and sausages, tins of rice pudding, a can opener and forks and spoons on the boat. They are useful when we decide to stay out longer than intended, or if the engine should break down. I always take a large packet of chocolate digestive biscuits on each trip to cheer us up when the fishing is slow or to celebrate a good catch. It is amazing how hungry you can get out there. Bottles of water are also carried, and extra warm clothing and waterproofs.

In sloppy seas, when driving to another mark, a rod leaning over the back of the transom may bounce overboard. On my boat, a rack would get in the way, so rods are stored flat inside the boat when not in use. If necessary, tie them down. It is handy to have a few pieces of thin rope. They need to be about 30in (76cm) long, with the ends melted and sealed to prevent fraying, as with all ropes.

You learn these tricks after precious rods and reels have disappeared over the side. I had a pair of Ambassadeur 7000s from the first batch that was ever made. After fifteen years they showed no sign of battle weariness, but on one trip they both vibrated out of their reel seats and were dumped overboard from the rod racks. Keep everything securely inboard, or you may lose it. Modern 7000s are just as good, but I had caught half a ton of cod off Dungeness on these two and almost as many bass off Beachy Head.

If you are launching a boat off the beach, everything needs to be totally secure and the boat must be completely seaworthy, even in the most calm weather. Sea fog clamps down rapidly, and while a small boat can follow a shore line, a compass makes everything so much easier.

I and some friends once had to drive 3 miles (5km) back to harbour in fog at night without a compass or anything else. We had only popped out for the evening and found ourselves enveloped in fog. The lights of the shore 200yds (183m) away were completely invisible. Fortunately a moon was intermittently glimpsed above us, so I kept it in the same position over my shoulder and followed a line of buoys back to the harbour.

OTHER KIT

Whether the boat is launched from a harbour, beach, or trailer, it requires a decent anchor. I use a folding one, to save space. It is like a grapnel, and 10ft (3m) of slim chain keeps it on the bottom up to the 50m line. Among rocks close to shore 20–30ft (6–10m) the chain is liable to snag, and I dispense with it.

The rope, or chain, is always fixed to the crown of the anchor, and a piece of twine is used to attach it firmly but breakably to the end of the stock. The rope needs to be about three times your likely depth. For emergency use, dispense with the twine and shackle the chain to the stock, so that the anchor cannot break out. If you are waiting to be rescued, let out 1yd (1m) of line every half hour, both for the tide and to prevent the rope chafing in one place. Put out enough rope to keep in position. If you anchor close to the rocks in a tide-race, drop the hook a long way up-tide so that

BOATING FOR BASS

Reels have a tough time offshore, but with regular maintenance and new line you can ensure they don't let you down at a critical moment.

you have room to manoeuvre. Never charge down-tide against a snagged anchor. You risk drowning yourself by swamping the boat so that it capsizes, or smashing off the transom.

Dan buoys are very good for marking the slot where the fish are feeding. I use a line of three small buoys to show the direction of the tide, each one 6ft (2m) apart. This is clipped to a thin rope, which goes to a tiny anchor and chain, and a large pick-up buoy is also clipped on ahead of it. The line ends with a loop. To retrieve the buoys, I slowly drive up-tide and alongside, on the down-wind side, hook the loop over a stern cleat, and motor up-tide. The large buoy slides down the rope and pulls out the anchor. The trick is to balance the weight of the chain so that it is a tad heavier than the anchor and stops it sliding back down to the sea-bed. The same trick can be used for hauling the boat's anchor.

The anchor for the dans can be dropped so that they end up floating alongside the mark, on the up-wind side, or marking the start of the drift. That may be a long way up-tide, so you need to know the compass bearing of the current flow to work out the correct angle, allowing for the wind and the way the tide is deflected by rocks or a wreck. In slack tides and calm seas, it is very hard to drift directly over some rocks and wrecks because they divide the water, and the boat slides off to one side of the hot-spot.

Drop the anchor gently so that nothing tangles. Do not drift over a dan line as the tackle inevitably tangles it, and you have either to chafe and snap your reel line, or reposition the buoys. It is often best to work on the down-wind side when dropping or pulling in anchors and buoys to avoid any chance of the boat blowing back over the rope and tangling it around the propeller.

My livebait tank is a 500l plastic water tank from a builder's merchant. It has been fitted with an overflow through the engine well, and there are boards around the inside to prevent tidal waves of water sloshing down the back of our legs. Whatever tank you use, do not overfill it, particularly in nasty seas, when it should be tied in place by a rope from the stern cleats. Mine is filled by a bilge pump mounted on a stainless-steel bracket outside the transom, below the water line. The water syphons back out of the tank, and the switch to refill it is located with all the others at the helm in front of me. It is a lot easier than buckets – although they are often handy.

BOATING FOR BASS

Because of the weight of the water, you may need to reduce the pitch of the propeller so that it bites less water and allows the engine to increase its power at the lower end of the scale. A low-pitch prop accelerates faster, which is handy when you have to do battle with big oncoming seas.

There are several other things to take care of. The floor needs to be non-slip. Carborundum dust or coarse clean sand can be sprinkled onto wet glass-fibre resin and paint. It sticks to the resin for years, but needs to be painted over again on wood with a second coat to support each grain.

The steering gear is best protected from the elements by a rubber boot. The helm should provide you with a decent work surface for tackling up, rebaiting, and noting down GPS numbers and fish finder details. A couple of foldaway deck-chairs are nice on a sunny day, if you have space. A bilge pump is useful to drain slops from the well, although the most effective bilge pump is a frightened man with a bucket – when the pump fails.

On each side of the cabin on my boat are pouches of trawl mesh held up with shock cord and strips of aluminium. These are secured to aluminium plates, which were drilled, countersunk, and roughed up, and had bolts stuck into place before being Sikaflexed into position. The pouches stop things bouncing around – things like tackle, life jackets, clothing, towels, ropes, the first-aid kit, flares, oil, grease and all sorts. There's a gaff hook on an old axe handle in there somewhere, and a paddle. All this is securely locked away behind a stout door with strong bolts and a hefty padlock.

Anti-fouling has to be done every year, and two coats usually last the season. The boat is scrubbed clean with a power washer, and sometimes it gets a lick of white paint inside – one-shot gloss seems perfectly adequate, especially as it has inbuilt fungicide. The outside was painted a year or so ago with a special two-part gloss paint, International Perfection 709, which costs a fortune, but which has renovated the tired old gelcoat. An old boat can be buffed up with a rubbing compound like T-Cut, then waxed to seal the pores. Quite severe damage to glass fibre can be repaired with some ease. It takes time, grinding, protective clothing and great cleanliness, but the results are both therapeutic and very strong.

A long-handled scrubbing brush keeps the boat ship-shape and smelling sweet in summer. We always squirt around some water, scrub it down, then mosey into the sea while the bilge pump empties the grime overboard. I put a cover on the boat when it is not in daily use, but a bit of rain water can be handy for giving the inside a scrub, adding some smelly kitchen cleaner to the water. Always make sure that everything works. Repair it the moment it doesn't, and keep a safe and tidy mooring.

A bilge pump, mounted on a bracket outside the boat, provides water for a livebait tank.

7 Fishing Offshore

It is a restless feeling, the night before a trip, as I stand in the garden, listening for the sound of surf breaking along the shingle bank half a mile away. A soft wind sighs through the fir trees, gentle on the land, but decidedly bouncy when fishing from a small boat far beyond the horizon. In the hollow stillness of the night, the stars gleam like diamonds over the sea. It will be a fine and early dawn, and the big bass will start feeding before sunrise. The hunger for lunker bass has me setting the alarm for 3.30 a.m., but the excitement makes sleep hard to find when the fish are running. How will the tide be – strong or feeble? Which way will the wind blow? Where will the bass be feeding? What baitfish are giving them an easy meal? The bass know precisely where to find them and as the years go by, the bass angler finds a pattern. Even so, it is a never-ending game of chess.

A double-figure bass used to be considered the fish of a lifetime. That was when we thought that bass spent their time close to shore or inside estuaries, and before specialist anglers came to understand the behaviour of this fish offshore. Some commercial anglers have caught dozens of 12–14lb bass. Nowadays we fish the old shipwrecks – and rusted hulks from the First World War that are full of caves and places for the bass to hide from

Many of the old wrecks are rusting away or being swallowed by sand. We could do with some new ones!

FISHING OFFSHORE

thresher sharks and porpoises. When fishing the wrecks, a ten or twelve pounder is the fish of the day, even if twenty gallons (75l) of fuel are required to catch it. Quite simply, bass fight so much better in the deep clear water offshore than when blinded by silty water inshore.

In summer, my world revolves around bass and weather forecasts, systems checks, deciding where to go, and keeping the boat, fishing tackle, and equipment in perfect working order. Bass fishing rules my life, and even as I drift off to sleep, I hear a fuel tank go 'clunk' in the garage as it shrinks with the cool night air.

The boat needs to be small to avoid frightening the fish, yet agile enough to handle heavy seas without danger. It bristles with aerials, and not just from a radio in case an accident befalls us – a fish finder pin-points individual fish; satellites pin-point the places where they feed. Where will that be tomorrow? Where will the lunkers be hitting the baitfish? Maybe they will be in ambush along a reef, or ganging up on the sprats and sandeels around a solitary rock or sandbank miles from land. Maybe they will be waiting around a wreck for dead or injured fish to come drifting past on the tide. Everything that the trawlers sweep back overboard – the pouting and all the undersized fish – end up somewhere. Many go down the gullets of large bass.

Wherever the bass may be, it's a 3.30 a.m. start. The alarm clock gives out an appalling electric shriek just when the body begs for the deepest sleep. After a bite of breakfast and a mugful of high-octane coffee, it's a short drive down to the harbour, half-awake. There is barely a word or grunt as my friend and I prepare the boat for the sea, but we are alert soon enough as the boat meets the open sea and the freshness of the dawn wind, slipping out through the harbour mouth as the north-eastern sky gleams brilliant blue and the sun comes up in a haze of mist pink behind the cliffs.

It is a fresh wind blowing warmth, but at this hour of the morning, with a 20 mile (32km) drive ahead, it is time to pull up the collar, face into the waves and open up the throttle. It is wonderful to go skimming out to the horizon on a calm morning, but when the sea is sloppy, the boat bucks and bounces over the waves. I have to steer around the lumpy bits, open up along the flat spots, or stop dead when a chasm suddenly appears ahead. The boat rides the lot, and the satellite navigator leads the way. As the sun heaves itself higher above the Downs, the world looks a lot friendlier. If everything goes to plan, and, in this game of chess, the right moves have been made, the promise of a fine day's sport can be seen from afar. A flock of feeding gulls is visible from several miles away, their wings flashing white in the early morning sunlight.

As the tide quickens, the baitfish get swirled about and the bass drive into them, stunning many, disabling others. They drift away with the tide, and the birds can see it it all happening from directly overhead. They see the sprats scattering in all directions and dive onto unwary ones swimming too close to the surface. It is better to arrive just as it is all starting, as the first herring gull dives in with a harsh shriek. Immediately ten more are on the scene, and a bunch of gannets. Within a few minutes, the gulls are wheeling and diving and the sprats throw out a wake on the surface as they scamper for safety. There's a heavy swirl amid the waves, and a roving bass turns looking for other helpless fish.

As the boat rides the tide and the rippling waves, line slips off the reel and the rubber eel streams astern. When a big bass is intent on getting its breakfast, it makes sure of it. The attack is violent – much more spectacular than its gentle tugging on the line when feeding inshore – but then the big ones have seen a bait or two.

FISHING OFFSHORE

Bass fight hardest in deep, clear water.

The best moment has to be when the boat is drifting on the waves and the gulls are diving in a squawking, squealing frenzy all around. Comes a savage thump. Without warning, the rod is suddenly dragged over as if the lure has just hit a solid brick wall. The reel screeches, the line sings in the freshening breeze, and you feel very much alive – the only boat in all those miles of heaving, gleaming sea.

Who knows how many will be down there? Tens? Hundreds? Some days the rod stays bent for as long as the arms can bear being jolted out of their sockets. Sometimes the bass have other plans. On those days, the early morning sun is harsh and brittle. The horizon is devoid of flickering wings, and the eyes feel gritty with all that staring and lack of sleep. I used to be up at dawn and out until dusk every day of the week, but I don't overdo it quite so much now. The brain becomes leaden, and memory fails. The addiction of bass fishing used to make a zombie out of me. Once I fell asleep beside the dance floor in a nightclub. The management thought I was drunk and threw me out. What did they know, or care, about the needs of hard-bitten bassmen!

It is an addictive sport, especially around the wrecks where massive bass are to be found. In mid-summer they are feeding hard and fighting fit. They smash into the lure and crunch the baitfish with amazing violence. You have to fight back, holding them hard to stop them diving into the wreck, and then fight them up to the boat. They certainly do fight, from the sea-bed, to the top, and back down again.

Bass move around a lot with the tides and weather, but they will be somewhere, on some tide, and we will catch up with them soon enough. All that is needed is a boatful of electronics and thirty years' experience. At the end of the day, as we head back to harbour, we admire the lunkers lying in the box. Bass don't just look handsome and fight like demons. They also taste delicious.

The only trouble with going a long way offshore is that *everything looks the same*. A flat sea cannot compete with the superb backdrops on some storm beaches. A twelve-pounder from a clear surf or rock ledge is a more worthy fish than a twelve-pounder from an offshore reef or wreck, purely on account of the scenery.

The surf and the rocks produce a lot of bass each season, but the periods when the fish are in front of you and feeding are comparatively brief. Once you have walked to your favourite mark and have spent a couple of hours fishing a chosen area, it is inconvenient to have to gather up your tackle and go trudging off to the next swim where, later in the tide, the bass may be found feeding again. A boat provides you with much greater mobility. It is no trouble at all to fish part of the tide in one mark,

121

FISHING OFFSHORE

This 9½lb bass took a mackerel bait intended for tope, and ignored the steel trace.

it were feasible. Standing in the surf is more fun because it is such a physical experience.

It is important to keep in touch with the fish, and the weather, in order not to miss any opportunities. My barometer hangs near the kettle, so that I can give it a tap every time I brew up. For the boat angler, work becomes a painful experience when the sea is flat and the sun is shining. I hate driving my car inland on days like this – they are too infrequent to waste. The greatest problem, earlier in the season, is the algal bloom, known around here as 'May-rot'. Ultimately it sinks, stratifies and blackens out the lower layer of the water column. It clogs everything: gills, ropes, nets and lines.

TACKLE

The same rods and reels that are used on the beach are equally useful from a boat for light legering, float fishing, spinning and fly fishing. However, large bass offshore often prove to be very powerful fish, and they require tackle that can tame them. For several seasons I have used Conoflex Integra rods, which come in various grades of power. These rods have an extendable butt. They can be used either as long conventional boat rods, or the butt can be extended so that they can be used for boat casting. The Integras have the power to control large fish, but are not so strong that middle weights cannot put up a good show. Rods need plenty of backbone to pump big fish against the current when fishing at anchor and must be able to hold lunkers out of wrecks when drifting. Whatever rod is used, it needs a decent reel seat and good rings. I am not over impressed by ceramic-lined rings. They cause a lot of friction with the line and are therefore less sensitive during the fight and when detecting bites.

I normally use Ambassadeur 7000 reels, but whatever reel you use, it must be strong-

go whizzing up the coast to the next mark, and then, perhaps, go far beyond the horizon to a third favoured location.

Besides being a mobile tackle box, a boat is no more than a convenient platform from which to fish – a mobile rock ledge! Many of the tricks and techniques that are useful from the beach can also be used to good effect from a boat, together with much of the tackle. Some minor adaptations may be necessary, but the main difference is that these tricks can often be used with greater precision.

However, without exception, surf fishing is impossible from a small boat. Rough seas and boats do not mix. Although I have heard of bass anglers fishing into the surf from behind the braking waves, stunts like this are dangerous and foolhardy. Besides, the whole point about surf is that it attracts the fish so close to land that there is no point in fishing from a boat, even if

FISHING OFFSHORE

A boat casting rod, such as this Conoflex Integra, has the power and flexibility to control hard-fighting lunkers.

ly made, compact, light in weight, easy to clean and balance well with the rod. The 7000 is the ideal all-round reel for use offshore. It has certainly stood the test of time. The design has reigned supreme for more than twenty years and is unlikely to be surpassed. I always rub a thin layer of water-proof grease inside the sideplates to keep the alloy free from corrosion. The gears are lubricated with heavy grease, the bearings with the same sticky oil that is used in the gearbox of my outboard motor. Like this, they last a season and require little extra maintenance.

Bass are often found close to heavy structure. Most wrecks are like huge old scrap heaps, and the line is easily damaged by rusty railings, girders, old hawsers, guns, lost trawl nets, and so on. My main line is 26lb breaking strain, and it often comes back severely chafed. I use white nylon as it becomes nearly invisible in water. For traces, I prefer 22lb line. A fluorescent, high-visibility line, like Stren, is useful for trolling and float trolling as it enables you to keep a close eye on the lines.

You can save time by making traces in preparation for the coming season. I use a pad of kitchen paper that has been dabbed with furniture wax to lubricate the line and assist knot tying. Some modern lines do not take kindly to the traditional drop of saliva before tightening the knot. Wind long traces around a block of plastic foam and store them in a wide-mouthed plastic jar with a screw lid to keep out the salt air.

I never carry an excess of tackle. Most of my fishing is accomplished with the same sort of kit that I have listed in the chapter on shore fishing: lines for traces of different breaking strains, a selection of hooks – up to 6/0 – and lead weights – 1–8oz (28–227g), swivels, elastic

FISHING OFFSHORE

A simple means of storing traces.

thread, and a selection of lures – spinners, pirks, plugs, Redgills, feathers and flies. A landing net is essential, and I prefer a large mesh one so that hooks are easy to untangle from it.

The priest on my boat is the glass-fibre butt spigot of a heavy-duty surf rod 14in (36cm) long. If the bass is not to be put back alive, kill it with a couple of sharp raps behind the eyes immediately after landing it. The fish has just had the biggest dose of fresh air in its life and is in shock. It should be unhooked and returned, or killed, before it comes out of shock and starts thrashing about in the bottom of the boat.

It is wise to carry extra warm clothing and overtrousers on board for people who come out in shorts and a T-shirt. A thick sweater or a bodywarmer is frequently useful. Sea breezes can become very chilly, and there is nothing worse than a cold, whingeing crewman who wants to go home just as the fish start feeding.

It is best not to allow weights or spools of line to rattle and roll around as the boat rolls. The noise becomes very irritating after a while. I place a towelling beer mat on the tackling-up shelf to prevent this. I do not leave mackerel banging around in the fish box, either. Lead weights should be restrained and not allowed to rattle and bang about while motoring up-tide to start the next drift. When fishing at anchor in calm, shallow water, nothing should be allowed to bang the hull and risk scaring the bass, be that a lead weight or a bass.

DRIFTING

Drifting is a useful technique when fishing ledges, reefs, sandbanks, wrecks and similar structure. It enables you to fish a large area and locate where the bass are lying. Once this has been established, the drift can be abbreviated, so that you fish directly to the feeding bass. However, this also runs the risk of frightening spooky fish. Usually, the best time to start drifting is an hour or more into the tide, when the fish have assembled to take advantage of food that is being swept towards them by the current. However, that is not always the only time because when the tide changes, everything has to move from one side of the reef or wreck to the other, to position itself for the changing current. A 1½ knot current seems to be ideal for bass to ambush their prey. It is not so fast as to carry off the bass and expose them to predators over the sandy wastelands.

124

FISHING OFFSHORE

Very often the presence of feeding bass is revealed by diving gulls and gannets. The cry 'The birds are working" is music to the bass angler's ears. The fish go into a feeding frenzy caused by the blood in the water. Each time a bass crunches a baitfish, it bursts the heart and gills. The smell and the activity draw other bass into the area. Whenever you see birds working, either investigate the place immediately, or make a note of the location. You do not need to see large numbers of birds working. I have caught a lot of bass through seeing just one gull dive down, or even aborting a dive. It spotted something down there, and anglers should investigate such sightings. They often prove to be reliable places for catching bass.

Lots of gulls sitting on the water often means a large shoal of mackerel 10ft (3m) below the surface, and the gulls are expecting them to drive the baitfish up to the surface at any moment. For some reason, a lone gull is often seen sitting immediately above a wreck, so if you cannot find it, give the place where the gull is sitting a thorough pinging with the fish finder. It is also worth noting flights of gulls heading in a specific direction at a particular state of the tide, especially during their breeding season. This usually means that they have located shoals of bass far from land and are going to feed on whatever baitfish are driven up to the surface.

Artificial lures, like Redgills and pirks, are ideal for fishing on the drift, and so too are plugs. In deep water, a pirk and a string of three Redgill Rascals are useful for searching the water. The gills are mounted on 4in (10cm) snoods, each one about 18in (45cm) apart, and the same distance to a 6–8oz (170–227g) pirk. Larger Redgills are also useful for drifting out deep, when a shoal of fish has been located, fished singly on a long trace. Plugs can be very effective inshore, when cast practically onto the beach from a drifting boat, but all this business is dealt with in the next chapter.

Herring gulls, blackbacks, and gannets are reliable indicators of bass. The gulls are often seen flying 70–100ft (20–30m) above the sea and scanning it. Smaller sea-birds, like terns, black-headed gulls and kittiwakes, feed on smaller fry, and their fluttering a few feet above the water usually signifies school bass, mackerel, or other predators.

Bass follow the baitfish, so if a structure is going to be any good, the mackerel, scad and pouting are already there. Years ago, a friend and I saw large shoals of mackerel boiling on the surface, thrashing the sea to foam. We did

A 17lb pollack. You can tell when you have hooked a 'stranger' because it stops fighting as it gets closer to the surface.

125

FISHING OFFSHORE

Gulls working over feeding bass on the ledge at Beachy Head.

not realize until some seasons later that those mackerel were not attacking fry, but were trying to escape the attentions of a shoal of lunker bass. We later learned that this particular mark is a lunker hot-spot and it has since yielded large numbers of 10–15lb bass. So, too, have several other places where we used to see plumes of gulls. We thought they were working over mackerel and ignored them for years.

Several of these marks have since given me bumper catches on livebaits. At the place where we saw the mackerel thrashing the surface to foam, my wife Sandra and I had our first expedition together. There was a huge shoal of bass beneath the boat. We were both into fish the moment we dropped our baits overboard. I ended up trying to fight my fish, rebait Sandra's line, net my fish and hers, and sort out the odd tangle – all at the same time. It was a hectic session, and we both had a few sharp words to say to each other in the almost constant confusion of it all, but we managed to catch twenty-eight bass averaging 8lb. It was certainly an afternoon to remember. We went back the next day, but most of the shoal had moved on. Even so, Sandra caught a ten-pounder – the best fish of the day. The most significant point about this mark is that it is a double ledge at the top of a bank. The bass lie in the hollow at the shallowest point, and sweep out to ambush passing baitfish. Double or multiple ledges, running across the tide, are very good places to find bass.

Another time, I fished a small wreck where I had often seen the birds working and where we had had a good catch a few days earlier. I invited a friend to come with me. It was an early start, and I waited for him on the dockside, but he did not turn up. I had to catch the tide, so I left without him. As I got to the wreck, gulls and gannets swarmed around, shouting abuse at me. The fish finder screen

FISHING OFFSHORE

side each other and the poppling interference in the ripple which reveals a school of fish.

I prefer to fish clear water offshore. Some cloudiness is acceptable, but fully transparent water is better. Finding the fish is the hard part, but a take means that you have discovered them. If it is a big shoal, fish can be caught on each drift. The best policy is to motor up-tide, giving the shoal a wide detour, and then drift back over it again. It would appear that each time you take a fish out of the shoal, none of the others notices anything alarming. Hungry fish are always at the front of the shoal; the ones that are not feeding are at the back. Often the largest bass are at the front and are the first to be caught.

A nine-pounder lies on the surface, thoroughly played out and ready for the net.

was a mass of fish symbols, so I could understand their irritation. The sea was quite sloppy that morning, with streaks of fog, but I found the wreck without trouble with my new GPS system (it is now obsolete!) I dropped my dan buoys and started fishing. Livebaits were hard to find, which was not surprising with all those bass around, but I caught enough to fish the tide. I discovered that the bass were eager to feed and soon my rod was bending into some very good fish. I ended up making my best-ever catch: twenty-five bass, three of them double-figure fish. Ever since then, my friend has not stopped asking me to take him fishing.

Wherever the bass and the birds go mad, a few fish can usually be found the following day. It takes several seasons to learn to read the gulls, and to glean information from the ripples on the sea, where currents flow along-

Double-figure bass are frequently encountered offshore.

FISHING OFFSHORE

LIVEBAITING

No predator likes to feel its dinner wriggling and jiggling around inside it, and bass usually kill their prey before swallowing it. Bass swim alongside baitfish like mackerel, just beneath it, then attack it with a sideswipe. They grab it across the gills, in the corner of their mouth, and crush it before swallowing. The heart is where the gills meet under the chin. Try crushing a dead mackerel's gills between your fingers and you will be amazed at how much pressure is needed to do so.

Mackerel, sprats and herring seem to have been designed to be crushed by bass. Their 'V'-shaped profile fits perfectly into the scissors at the corner of the bass's jaw. If you inspect a livebait after a bass has crunched its gills, you can see the scratches from its teeth. These may seem puny, but they have more strength than we appreciate because bass have no trouble killing their prey.

Some years ago I was trying to catch mullet in the harbour at Kinsale, in Ireland. They were not interested, so I tied on a fry-type reservoir lure, squeezed a couple of swan shots onto the line ahead of it, and dangled it in the water in front of me. Several mackerel and launce attacked it, and I was given a graphic demonstration of how they strike at a small fish. They all swam alongside, then side swiped the head.

Practically any fish that swims can be used as a livebait, but it is important to 'match the hatch', and give the bass what they are looking for, whether it is sandeel, a pouting, or a mackerel. When drifting with livebaits, I rig up a running leger tackle, even though the weight only touches the bottom once after being dropped down. The trace needs to be no more than 6ft (2m) long, or the bait may look too lively and the bass will not bother to chase it. Keep the tips of the rods as far apart as possible so that the traces do not tangle together.

A twitching livebait turns on the fish. If it is nearly dead it is highly catchable, and this spurs them into the attack. You can tell if bass are around a wreck or reef when the livebait starts panicking. This can often be felt on the rod-tip before a fish strikes and tries to drag the rod from your hands. Bass are not on all wrecks and reefs all of the time, but move about with the tides. The biggest structures often turn out to be their last refuge on very big tides.

When fishing livebaits, you can often feel small bass punching at the bait. Sometimes one takes it, and turns out to be little larger than the joey it has just tried to swallow. We have had them fall off the hook at the side of the boat, then take the bait again when it has been dropped back to them. Big bass swallow the bait and go, or dive for the bottom if they throw the hook.

The only way to fight a very large bass when drifting a wreck is to put both thumbs on the reel spool and hold it hard, playing the fish on your wrists and the rod, yielding as little line as possible unless the pressure looks like popping the line. Otherwise, the bass is likely to dive back into the structure and snap the line. Wait until the fish finder shows the wreck passing behind the boat, then allow the fish to have its head in snag-free water. After all, it is so nice to hear the reel screech when a big fish takes line against the drag. Big fish have to be 'pumped' up to the boat by lifting them in the water with the rod, then winding the tip back down and lifting again.

Make the bass fight the rod. It should always arrive at the boatside played out and too tired to offer further resistance. A bass thrashing at the surface is trying every possible angle to throw the hook, so a taut line is essential. Wind off the drag when the fish is close to the boat because it is quite likely to dive two or three times.

In deep water, bass are rarely found where the tide is boiling behind a wreck, reef or

A perfect surf on a beautiful beach in Pembrokeshire.

A scrapping eight-pounder caught from an offshore reef.

Double-figure bass eat large items of prey, like this mackerel.

Bass are now heavily exploited by commercial angling boats.

Using a cast net to catch whitebait.

A nice bass taken on Redgill and light tackle. On this occasion they hit the lure the moment I stopped winding.

Waiting for bites in a rolling Irish surf.

A brace of five-pounders from the surf on a rocky coast line.

Baits for bass (opposite).

Netting a bass taken on light tackle and a Redgill.

Ron Preddy with a ten-pounder: we have made several outstanding catches together.

In the old days, we coloured the Redgills ourselves. Now they are available in a wide range of attractive colours.

With ragworms in an aerator, fresh bait is readily available.

Netting a bass on the ledge at Beachy Head.

Seine netting for sandeels – a highly versatile bait.

A nice bass and a conger caught from a shallow reef.

Fishing a fillet of mackerel over an inshore reef at dusk, using chopped up mackerel for groundbait.

FISHING OFFSHORE

When drifting reefs and wrecks, the fish are often found in a very narrow slot. Unless the angle of the drift is spot-on, nothing will be caught. This has been brought home to me on many occasions, but none more vividly than last year when my regular fishing partner, Carl, and I were drifting a tiny wreck which lies along the tide. The hulk is on its side, partly buried in the sand, and the decks have rusted and collapsed. The fish are in the cave on the deckward side of the wreck, but the other side is nothing but steel plates and hull. As we drifted along it, Carl was fishing the open side, from his side of the boat, and hooked three ten- to eleven pounders on three consecutive drifts. I had to be content with a five-pounder.

LEGERING AND UP-TIDE CASTING

Several techniques can be employed from an anchored boat. The secret is to creep up on your mark and drop the anchor quietly so as not to spoil your chances before starting to fish. One of my favourite methods is to cast a bait on a 4ft (1.2m) trace about 30–50yds (27–46m) down-tide, depending on the depth of the water, and attract the fish with groundbait. I then put the reel into gear, wind off the drag, and snap on the click mechanism while waiting for a take. The drag can be adjusted to match the strength of the tide, so that there are no irritating false alarms.

In deeper water, up-tide casting places the bait beyond the boat's zone of disturbance. I make a simple paternoster tackle, without swivels. The lead link is joined to the main line with a four-turn water-knot (like a granny knot but with four turns through the loop). While fishing for plaice I have often used very long traces – up to 20ft (6m) – in this manner. A clip controls the baited hook for cast-

Go on – take it.

sandbank, but can usually be found some distance up-tide of the structure. In shallow water close to shore, they are more often found behind the cause of the disturbance, particularly if the current is brisk and the structure offers them shelter. Bass are often located in a small area, so it is vital not to bang around. Make a wide detour, then try another drift through the same area. When fishing shallow water, never drive over the mark you intend to fish. The same applies to hard-fished wrecks and reefs in deep water. The big, old bass take fright, and head for cover.

FISHING OFFSHORE

Bass of 10lb and 12lb, caught shortly before dawn.

FISHING OFFSHORE

ing, and the knot can be wound onto the reel. When casting up-tide of wrecks and reefs, I generally fish with mackerel strips, 8ft (2.4m) traces and bait clips.

Quite a heavy weight is sometimes advantageous, with fixed wires to jolt home the hook when a fish takes the bait. Light breakaway leads tend to break out and go trundling down-tide, giving the angler a big loop of slack line to reel in, and the bass often ejects the bait before the angler can catch up with it. An alternative is to whack the bait a long way down-tide using a lighter lead, either plain or a breakout, depending on the ground and the depth.

When fishing at anchor, very big bass exhibit a sense of strategy in the way they fight, and no doubt it has enabled quite a few of them to snap the line and escape. The fish swims up-tide of the boat, and then it turns and accelerates down-tide in a head-long dive. When a fish is close to the boat, it may have two or three more runs left in it, so I always slacken off the drag in case it wants to continue the fight at close range. This is a dangerous time, when the hookhold may have been torn, the line and trace may have become frayed, and when a strong fish may still be full of unstoppable power. Head-long dives in deep water are best dealt with by a moderate drag. The fish will not go very far – about 30ft (9m) – but the scream of the drag washers will ring in your mind for life.

Float fishing is another useful technique over wrecks and reefs. I fix a long strand of nylon between the float and a swivel which runs on the main line. It is stopped by a small bead and stop knot. Live or dead baits can be used, trotting them through the swim. Usually the fish are close to the sea-bed, so a fairly heavy weight is needed to drag the bait down to their level. This requires quite a large float, but it allows you to control the bait as it drifts with the tide.

TROLLING

Trolling artificial lures like Redgills and plugs is an effective technique, particularly in shallow water. The lures are streamed astern and are slowly towed behind the boat at a speed which permits them to work effectively and induce the fish to strike. It is a very good technique for finding the places where bass lurk in ambush, but a quiet engine is essential or the bass will take fright. An electric trolling motor is ideal.

I have spent a lot of time trolling for bass. In one place the boat is allowed to move slowly along, up-tide of a submerged ledge. The bass lie on the far side, and the boat ends up being pushed crabwise along the ledge by a combination of the tide and the engine. The boat is one side of the ledge, and the Redgills fish the other side. Sometimes the boat does not move, and the current works the lures.

I dislike using lead weights up-trace of the lure, even when a long trace is in use. Weights tend to dive for the sea-bed and snag up at the least opportunity. The minimum amount of weight should be used. A small spiral or a tubular weight is usually sufficient.

In deeper water, down-riggers are useful because they take the place of the weight, and the lures can be set to fish at a precise depth. A down-rigger is merely a heavy weight on a separate line, with a clip to take the reel line. The fish pulls the line out of the clip and usually hooks itself in the process.

I have two rod rests at the stern of my boat which allow the rods to project out over the water, like out-riggers. They prevent the lines from tangling. When turning the boat for the next pass, make a wide turn to avoid tangling the lines. When a fish is hooked, and the boat is stopped while playing the fish, the other lure needs to be reeled in or it may sink and snag the bottom.

FISHING OFFSHORE

Float trolling over an inshore reef, using long rods as outriggers.

This is unlikely to happen with a float-trolled livebait. This trick works best in shallow water, with the bait set to swim in mid-water. The line does not run directly to the float. I prefer to use a sliding float, but with a length of line between the float and a small swivel running on the line. This enables me to strike directly into the fish, rather than through the angle of the float, if it were fixed directly to the line. Overactive livebaits can be fished paternoster style, with the trace coming off the line, and the sinker at the end, beneath the bait.

Whatever style of fishing you enjoy most, it pays to develop a grapevine. I spend a lot of time gathering intelligence and spying through binoculars from the clifftops when I take the dogs for a walk. I have entered my spy-point into my GPS. It has permitted me to read off the distance and bearing of all the known marks. It helps to know the speed, hull design, and range of local bassmen.

A lot of useful information can be gathered from other anglers, harbour workers, longshoremen, tackle dealers, fish merchants, charter skippers, trawlermen, and anybody else who takes an interest in the comings and goings of other bass fishermen. However, be warned: most harbours and shore stations are awash with disinformation when the fish are running. The truth frequently has to be disentangled from a mass of exaggeration and downright lies!

8 Lures

The greatest fun is to be had from trying to persuade bass into thinking laterally. The only problem is that their sense of self-preservation makes them increasingly sceptical of lures, but therein lies the challenge. One of the biggest thrills in bass fishing comes with catching them in shallow water on artificial lures. In clear seas, bass of any size attack and fight like demons, providing magnificent sport. If the tackle is matched to the size of fish available, even schoolies put up a good show, and indignantly dash away when they are slipped back into the sea. Bass that are hitting baitfish fight with all their power when caught in clear, shallow water. They are less encumbered by a fly, spinner or plug than by a lead weight. Hooked fish make several runs, especially when they find themselves being pulled ever closer to the edge or to the side of a boat.

One of the best things about catching bass on artificials is the take. The lure is stopped dead in its tracks as if it has hit the proverbial brick wall. There is a brief pause as angler and bass realize they are hooked into each other, then the rod plunges over as the bass powers away on its first run.

Bass are most likely to hit lures in clear water, when they can see where they are going. Cloudy water produces fish, but clear is better because the fish can see the bait from

Rock ledges are ideal for spinning and plug fishing.

LURES

This nine-pounder fell for a single feather.

farther away. I often watch them hunting around Beachy Head Ledge, and they sweep into the attack with amazing speed, scattering the baitfish in all directions. They have very good eyesight.

I envy anglers who fish around granite and sandstone. They don't have chalk cliffs and muddy seas, and bass are often seen swirling and hunting close inshore. It is amazing how fast a chalk fall dissolves into the sea and how much the ensuing silt gets stirred up by the lightest summer breeze. I have absolutely no doubt that bass prefer to hunt baitfish in clear water, although they have no problem coping when they are overtaken by rough weather and cloudy water. Shore marks where the sea is normally clear are, however, more likely to feature on their map than areas where the water is usually murky, unless it holds plenty of crab.

Lures have to be fished with intense concentration and sensitivity. The bass need to be convinced that your scrap of metal, wood, rubber, or tinsel is actually a live fish, so you have to be aware of how to fish it so that it looks its best. The starting point is knowing how much line the reel retrieves with each turn of the handle, and therefore how fast the lure is swimming, according to its weight and design, the current speed and depth of water.

Lures are inert. Only the angler can teach them to swim and, in so doing, convince bass that they are alive and worth attacking. They should not look too healthy. There needs to be a balance between too much movement and an easily attacked meal. Some anglers fish lures much too fast. The idea is to represent an injured baitfish, and they certainly do not rush around the ocean. Slow and very slow retrieves are usually most successful, but a sudden burst of acceleration often produces a violent response.

It is not uncommon, after snagging up and pulling the lure clear of weed, for a bass to come hurtling out of nowhere and seize it as it comes flying out of the water. This is quite spectacular, especially when the fish is close. If it misses, continue retrieving normally, or make another cast and it will probably attack again with equal vengeance. At nearly every other time, it is best to make the lure dart, then half topple along, like a very sick baitfish.

When casting across a current from the shore or casting to one side from a drifting boat, predators often take a lure as it changes direction and comes towards you. You have to be careful when fishing plugs, spinners and large flies offshore as gulls sometimes swoop down and seize them.

Plug fishing and spinning are excellent ways of searching a shore line for where the fish hang out. The tackle and the technique are so simple: just walk along the beach, casting ahead of you. When the sea is clear and clean, keep off the skyline and out of sight, or the fish will be frightened before they can take the lure. Wear clothing that blends into the background. If you are wading in calm conditions, do not slosh through the water, sending out a bow-wave, or the bass may think a seal is after them and quit the area. Start by casting along the shore line, then fan the casts out to sea so as not to disturb the shallows before fishing them. A good time is when the sea is slightly choppy, with clear water and a gentle onshore breeze.

Few beaches are sufficiently deserted to allow bass to get into the habit of patrolling the shore line undisturbed, but they do move inshore late in the evening and at night, and are often caught early in the morning. Bass, like trout, patrol sandy shallow areas after dark and at dawn.

Bass come nosing around the edge of the rocks in very calm water. This is a good time for drifting close in to the cliffs and casting inshore. Often it is the only way to avoid being cut off by the tide. Bass concentrate inshore, on the edge of currents which are forcing small fish to find shelter. Baitfish are easy to catch when the bass chase them into the tide.

You should always keep your eyes peeled for diving sea-birds, sandeels being hit, or the swirls and flashes from attacking bass. Watch out for the popple on the surface caused by a school of bass, or mullet – or any other fish just under the surface. If bass start following the lure, try a much smaller one. It sometimes induces the fish to attack.

Watch for followers, shapes, small fish jumping out of the way, and other signs of predatory activity. Even when fish are not caught, all such events should be correlated with the tide, time and weather and noted in your fishing diary. In years to come, this information will prove invaluable. Ultimately a pattern will take shape and a serious truth of bass fishing lore will emerge. Thus, you learn how to be in the right place at the right time.

Unfortunately, bass are not the only fish that seize lures. They produce a by-catch of mackerel, wrasse, pollack and some other varieties. At least they don't catch dogfish and eels!

Spinning over a shallow reef offshore.

LURES

TACKLE

Rods

For spinning and plug fishing I prefer to use a light rod of 10–11ft (3–3½m) with a test curve around 2lb and a steely backbone. A long rod enables you to steer the lure through weed-beds and around boulders, and to impart a fish-like action to the lure. Carp rods are excellent and are also useful for float fishing with baits like prawn, and for fishing the bottom in light surf or from the rocks. Plugs are not aerodynamic, and a rod with a bit of power is needed to whack them into a breeze. A rod with some backbone is essential for banging home the hooks. Attacking bass grip a lure solidly, and it has to be dislodged from its grip before the hooks can sink home, preferably in the scissors.

A few seasons ago, Ron Preddy and I came across a shoal of feeding bass behind a rock ledge. Sea-birds were diving in, so I hastily anchored the boat (by the stern!) so we could try a few casts. We only had mackerel spinning rods, and the 3–4lb bass that we caught fought like crazy. As the tide strengthened, much bigger fish (7–8lb) came along, but we could not hook them with our flimsy rods. We had several almighty takes, but after bending our rods double, the fish let go. Even so, we landed the best part of two dozen bass to 6lb.

The flash of a high-gloss rod in bright sunlight can spook fish, so it is best to matt down the varnish by gently rubbing it with a scouring pad. You might try side-casting, if necessary, to keep the rod off the skyline. Large rings reduce friction when fishing with fixed-spool reels. Ceramic-lined rings offer so much friction that they tend to grip the line. Most rings are brilliant nowadays, but any that show signs of grooving, cracks or wear, especially at the tip, must be changed before they can chafe or damage the line. Sliding reel seats are of little use when spinning or plugging as they have an irritating habit of coming loose during the fight and allowing the reel to fall off. A screw-up reel seat is much more secure and locks the reel tightly onto the rod.

Reels

For general fishing, I use fixed-spool reels loaded with 10lb line. Multipliers can be used, but an aerodynamic lure weighing at least ½oz (14g) is needed to set the spool spinning. It is much more likely to overrun when casting plugs and similar bulky lures that catch the wind.

Many models of fixed-spool reel are beautifully designed. The best ones are light, compact, saltwater-proof, have a roller line pick-up and a smooth-running drag. Some anglers prefer to fight fish by back-winding rather than through the drag. I prefer to use the drag because the slightest mistake when the rod is being doubled over by a lunker can lead to a tremendous bird's nest and a lost fish. If the drag control is at the back of the reel, it can be adjusted during the fight. Finger pressure on the side of the spool is often necessary when landing a fish. The pressure can be released immediately if the bass runs again.

Lines

The line most commonly used is 10lb; 8lb is a bit light for fishing among snags, so I sometimes use 12lb line. Fortunately bass are not particularly line shy, but heavy line requires more weight for casting. Dyneema line should be useful for lure fishing, as it would enable perfect control of the lure, and easy hook setting.

End the line with a small link swivel so that the lure can be changed easily. The link

LURES

A played-out seven-pounder is easy to land on a pirk. This one is fitted with a single hook.

LURES

should permit the lure to swim freely and not hold it at an angle away from the line and spoil its action. The golden rule of lure fishing is to beware of the stress of casting. It tightens up knots to the point of self-destruction. It is best to retie the knot after every twentieth cast, or sooner if you are catching good fish, because a hefty bass may smash the line like flimsy cotton. The final few feet should always be checked after pulling out of a snag.

I prefer to use lures that have sufficient inbuilt weight for casting. Up-trace lead weights wreck the action of plugs, spinners and rubber eels, making them swing about. Baitfish do not swim in a zig-zag from top to bottom, but keep a remarkably steady line.

Other Kit

In warm weather, some anglers go fishing in shorts and trainers and wet wade. It is worth taking a light water-proof jacket and trousers in case the weather changes. A small box is handy for carrying plugs and spinners when you are ambling over the rocks or along the beach and casting here and there. I use the boxes that video-tapes are packed in. Plugs, spinners and Redgills are prevented from rattling around by a layer of plastic packing material. It is important to look after lures and keep them away from dirt and corrosion. It is also a good idea to fit the treble hooks with guards, or they will tangle together.

Whether spinning, plugging or fly fishing, Polaroids and a peaked hat reduce glare and allow patrolling bass to be spotted and cast to. Glasses and a hat eliminate the chance of getting the hook of a fly embedded in your scalp or, worse, your eye.

Lures

One of the handy things about lure fishing is that they are always available and can be acquired at any time. Trusty old favourites can be restored and re-armed in the winter: check the mountings, split-rings and hooks to avoid losing big fish.

You do not need the most complicated of lures. My wife Sandra once caught a bass through a hole in the staging at Eastbourne pier, using silver foil on the hook and her dad's wrist watch as a weight. The bass were feeding on whitebait, and Sandra was 'matching the hatch'. This is important, particularly when the bass are feeding on sandeels, pouting, poor cod or wrasse, rather than on mackerel or herring.

I feel most confident when using colours that match the baitfish: blue and silver and green and silver when sandeels, herring and mackerel are the prey. Black and silver also works well, and a golden-silver colour is a handy shade in the autumn when the bass are feeding on whiting, pouting and poor cod. I have a suspicion that as bass attack from beneath, the colour of a lure's belly may be significant. If it looks white, like bass, the fish may not take it. Pollack are sometimes unwilling to take golden coloured lures, so this may be why. My reasoning is that if there was a dearth of baitfish, the predators might start hitting their own fry, which is not usually how nature goes about its business.

A confusion of lures is unnecessary – just two or three types that you know how to fish, in different sizes. Lures are dead objects. Dangle them in the water, and they will not catch anything. Only the angler can impart life and movement to them. He has to understand how they perform and how to fish them. The thinking that drives them matters much more than the style or design. Every successful lure fisherman trails his offering through the water before casting it out, checking on the action and watching how it swims to his feet during the retrieve. You have to think them through the water.

LURES

SPINNING

I have caught bass by trolling along a reef, with the boat one side of a ledge and a Redgill wafting along the downtide edge where the bass are waiting in ambush. A hooked fish is sometimes followed by others, and I have often caught another fish by casting a spinner and retrieving it slowly. It is always worth holding a fish for a while for this purpose. I have also discovered it is much less hassle to anchor up with the stern of the boat above the lip of the reef and spin along it.

Spinning is a very good technique for exploring a shore line. Rocks, reefs, weed beds and jetties all produce fish but open expanses of steep shingle beach can also be productive. A friend of mine catches bass and sea trout by walking along the shingle at high water in September, when lots of bait fish are close to shore. The period between first light and sunrise is the best time to fish.

A slow retrieve usually catches most fish, so it is important to match the weight and profile of the spinner to the current speed and depth of water. For example, the trusty 1oz (28g) ABU Toby comes in different thicknesses. The thin version can be fished more slowly than the thicker one, which sinks more quickly. As always, you need to feel the spinner coming through the water and imagine how lame it looks to a bass.

Another old favourite, the ABU Koster, is a compact lure. It casts very well, but it does not have as much grip on the water. It sinks fairly fast, so it needs to be fished quickly or in a current, where the water is more likely to support it. Both this and the Toby look like sprats, which my local bass attack at every opportunity. Sprats are easily crippled by bass and are feeble swimmers at the best of times, so lures that represent them should be fished slowly.

The German Sprat is a long-established bass lure and is nowadays marketed as the Cebar. Its slim profile permits it to sink quickly, so it needs to be fished fairly fast or in deeper water to avoid snagging. It casts well, and is good for fast currents. When the fish are close to the surface or in shallow water, stop the line flowing from the reel when the spinner is 10ft (3m) above the water so that it does not sink far before you start fishing it.

When the bass are playing hard to get, it is often a good idea to jiggle the rod as you

For many years, Abu Garcia has made a wide selection of highly effective spinners for bass.

LURES

A large Mylar feather looks like a sprat in the water, and fishes best on a long trace.

retrieve the lure, or to move the tip from side to side when the lure is getting close, so that it imitates a sick or injured fish, changing direction rather than following one line.

The Toby, Koster, Cebar and Big S spinners have accounted for thousands of bass over the years, but when the fish are feeding, the type of spinner is of less consequence than the colour, action, and size. Most of the time the 1oz (28g) versions are most useful, particularly when casting into a wind or when you are searching a wide area. The lighter versions are useful when the fish are striking small baitfish, or when the bass persist in following the lure.

PLUG FISHING

Spinning becomes a frustrating business in shallow water and when a lot of floating weed is around, or thin green strands are reaching up from the bottom in shallow water. This is where plugs come into their own. They were once considered to be useless for sea fishing, rather like pirks when they were first introduced into this country. However, expert bass anglers like Dr Mike Ladle rediscovered them and developed their use in the sea. Now they are a standard part of the bass angler's armoury.

Floating plugs are ideal for shallow reefy water because they float out of trouble if you stop the retrieve and avoid the snags. The steepness with which they dive can be adjusted by setting the angle of the lip. The shallower the angle, the deeper they dive. Sinking plugs are useful in deeper water, but spinners are generally better in these conditions. It is unwise to throw an expensive lure into unknown waters where it might sink to the bottom and refuse to let go. As usual, it is best to work plugs slowly so that they look lame and easy to mug. This is not very straightforward in a swift current, even when using a sinking plug, as the action becomes too fast.

Plugging is a mobile form of fishing, and an interesting way of sussing out unknown territory. You have only to walk along the beach, looking for the larders and the ambush points where bass are most likely to be found, and make some exploratory casts to see what happens. Each cast brings fresh hope, until suddenly a bulge appears on the surface behind where the plug is fishing, hopefully followed by a heavy swirl as the bass strikes it, rather than a flash of the gills and a boil as it misses or rejects the lure. Bass investigate clumps of weed, piles of boulders and similar snaggy areas where baitfish hide.

The great advantage of a plug is that you can cast it into the most snaggy swims and

LURES

tease it through a clump of weed stems and boulders. If it snags up hard, and no amount of coaxing persuades it to free itself, spare the rod and reel. Wind the line around your sleeve or a bit of wood, walk slowly backwards and hope the hook cuts itself free.

When a large grey torpedo suddenly materializes behind the plug, and persists in following it, a take can sometimes be induced by tweaking the lure through a clump of weed, between two boulders, or out of clear water into dirty water. The bass may only be following, but it does not want its prey to escape, and may be induced into striking at the last moment. This is also a good reason for standing (or squatting) a little way back from the sea and fishing the bait right up to the water's edge. Most plug fishing is done at close range because plugs are anything but aerodynamic and can rarely be cast much further than 40yds (37m) – even less distance into a breeze.

One of the best times to fish these lures is when bass are investigating little bays at first light. They are often extremely close to shore. Another good time is in the afternoon, at high water, when the shore line has been warmed by the sun. Fishing is often good under cliffs, which reflect heat into the water. It is usually easiest to fish from a boat at high tide, keeping 50yds (46m) out from the edge, and landing the plugs on the rocks if necessary. It helps if you can use an electric trolling motor to stay on the right line.

Plug fishing works well at night when the fish are close to shore. They see the silhouette darting above them. Matt black plugs are most effective for this purpose, and it is easy to spray up one or two for night fishing. A black night is fine, but moonlight is better, with thin cloud to make the sky white. A background of sea front or harbour lights also enables the fish to locate the lure. They can see the plug clearly against it. Perhaps they pick up the vibrations on their lateral line, which may be why they prefer calm, shallow water for hunting.

Plugging works well around harbours and estuaries. A lot of bass visit these places at night, hunting for crabs, small fish and manky old pouting thrown overboard from trawlers. Most harbours have nooks and crannies that are attractive to bass, and the lights from harbourside installations show the silhouette of any baitfish that is foolish enough to leave cover.

Do not try to land a fish that has a mouthful of treble hooks by taking hold of its gill cover, or you may end up being attached to it.

This six-pounder hit the plug with typical aggression.

LURES

Plugs like these have caught a lot of bass in recent years.

A thrashing bass with a mouthful of hooks can be dangerous, as many anglers have had time to consider while waiting in the Emergency Room of a hospital for hooks to be removed from their thumbs. It is better to use a landing net with a large mesh, as it is relatively easy to disentangle hooks. Knitted mesh nets and treble hooks are a nightmare. Unhook the fish with forceps or long-nose pliers. Fish that are to be returned should be wrapped in a wet towel so they cannot thrash about while being unhooked.

Treble hooks are essential for balancing plugs so that they stay upright and swim with the correct motion. A vast amount of research goes into designing plugs. Some people replace the treble hook on spinners with a single hook, but that is not advisable with plugs, even though most bass are caught on the hook that hangs from the plug's belly. The only times I have fished plugs in deep water – 100ft (30m) they have tangled the main line, despite using a 'flying collar' rig, and I have caught zilch. A down rigger might be useful, but that seems too complicated for deep water where pirks and Redgills are usually most effective.

Hunting bass generally have plenty of time to inspect a plug, so the colour should match the baitfish they are seeking. When they are looking for wrasse around reefs, use a plug that is green-bronze, like a small ballan wrasse, or paint one to look like a cork wing wrasse. A 3½in (9cm) plug that is coloured golden-yellow is most likely to be taken by bass that are hunting small pouting and poor cod; similarly, pollack coloured plugs, fished close to rock faces and pier pilings.

Most plug-caught bass are caught on floating, jointed plugs. The bass agree that these have the best action, but many others work too. Ones to consider are as follows: Rebel J30 and J30S (sinker); Rapala J9, J11, J13 & J15, CD7, Magnum, and Slim 13; Diawa Flipper; Jensen 25; Shadman; Bomber 16, 17 J and the Bomber Long A. This list is not finite and new plugs come onto the market all the time. Home-made plugs are not often as effective as commercial patterns, which are better designed and extensively researched, but you can repaint them with more fish-like colours to match the baitfish that the bass are preying on. Having said that, how about making a 'drowning rat' plug? It should work around harbours and sewer outfalls.

REDGILLS

Bass find Redgills irresistible. One of the good things about this lure is that it is so versatile. In its various sizes, it can be fished in a variety of ways. The silver-blue and silver-green are best, and I like the dappled shade that looks like a mackerel, with a wide tail that swims seductively. I paint eyes on mine, and attach tufts of red wool, to make them look like damaged gills. I think they catch more fish like this. I also fish them on fairly thick line. It acts like a parachute in the water and helps to support the larger sizes of Redgill.

This lure can be trolled from a boat, using a long trace to the Redgill and a quick-release drilled bullet or two, 15–20ft (4.5–6m) from the lure, to take it down to the fish. Plugs can be fished this way, too. One of the best times is around low water, when the fish are congregated by the tide, trolling the lures at walking speed 150yds (137m) astern and close in to the beach, or over the tops of reefs farther offshore.

Most anglers prefer to cast Redgills. Some weight is required, but not an up-trace lead, which spoils the action in shallow water. Some anglers wrap lead wire around the hookshank to give casting weight. It is best to glue each layer of wire into place. Rig the Redgills with strong nylon, and tie a small swivel at the nose so that they can be clipped onto the line like spinners and fished in a similar manner and circumstances. They are great lures to fish where the birds are working, and the bass often hit them very solidly. It can also be productive to trail a Redgill under mackerel shoals. Look after your Redgills and treat them properly as they hardly ever attract fish when they spin or twirl through the water.

From the boat, I rig Redgills with a 6–12ft (2–4m) trace which is tied to a swivel. A weight

The Redgill has a mighty reputation as a catcher of bass, and comes in many appealing colours and sizes.

LURES

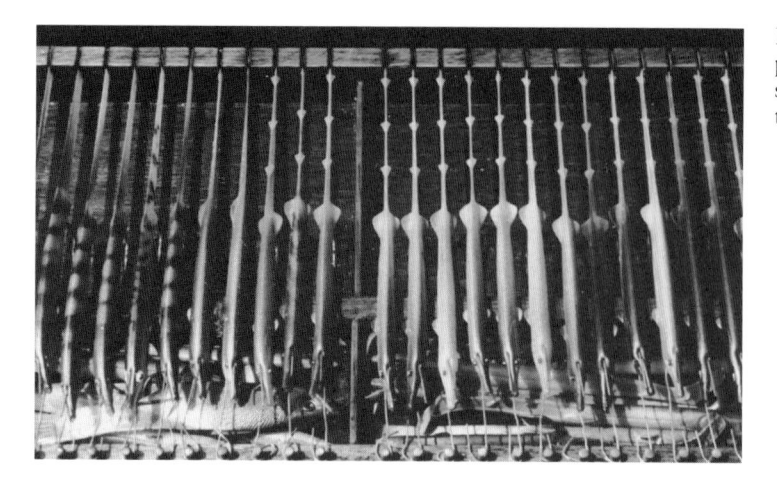

Redgills have to be stored properly to keep their tails straight, or bass will refuse them.

is clipped to the opposite end of the swivel, alongside the reel line. This can be cast a fair distance and does not tangle. Drop the Redgill into the water before flicking it away from the boat. There is rarely any need to cast far. I prefer this method to a 'flying collar' rig, which uses an 'L' shaped wire boom. I cast out to one side of the drifting boat and let the Redgill sink to the sea bed before starting to work it.

After the weight has hit bottom, start winding slowly. I always count the turns: four slow winds, three fast ones – a 6ft (2m) dash – then slow again. In deep water, I count up to twenty five, unless the fish finder or swirls denote that the bass are close to the surface. One evening, at the top of each winding session, I raised the rod tip and let the Redgill drift for a second or two. Each time, I felt a tiny tap – almost insignificant – and wound into a thumping lunker. I caught several bass like this, and yet I have never known them to take like that since.

From the boat, note the direction of the wind and tide. If the wind is faster than the tide, or blowing against it, the eel may be working fast enough without extra help. Redgills also work well when they are allowed to swim in a current, keeping stationary. This does not seem to strike the bass as unusual.

Some people use the Jif lemon trick, casting out with a Jif lemon bottle filled with wax. A 4ft (1.2m) trace goes to a small Redgill. It casts well and floats across the current. It is used to catch school bass from some swift, snaggy, shallow swims, but this is not a trick I would recommend.

I do most of my fishing with the 178mm Redgill Raver, but the smaller 115mm Redgill Rascal is also effective. Some anglers use little 90mm Delta sandeels, and in recent years anglers have had success with wobbling plastic worms, like Mister Twisters.

PIRKING

Bass hit pirks very hard when they are in a feeding frenzy, and if the split rings holding the hook and swivel are not strong, lunker bass snap them easily, as I have found to my cost. This is mainly a boat fishing technique, although some anglers fish them in deep water along the side of piers.

Small, slim pirks work well, and they can easily be made at home from lengths of 15 mm stainless steel tube, filled with lead. Other heavy lures, like the Hopkins Hammerhead are just as effective. Generally, pirks weighing

LURES

Most designs of pirk catch bass.

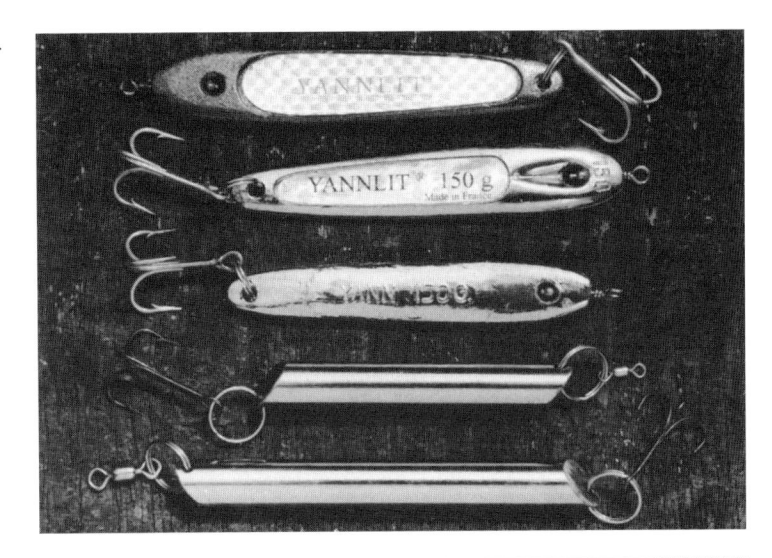

Making pirks in a can of dry sand.

6–12oz (170–240g) are best. The way to fish them is to jig them close to the bottom, or trail them through a shoal of fish. Often, while reeling in fast to avoid a snag, I have had bass hit them with great ferocity.

A pirk and a string of three Redgill Rascals, or large feathers, is a commercial method of catching shoaling bass. Multiple hooks-ups are frequent, which is not sporting. A single pirk is much more fun.

FLY FISHING

When you reach for the fly rod, you realize that the sea is a very large place. There is a lot of it to cover and usually the breeze is coming from an awkward angle. However, fly fishing with a reservoir-type outfit is perfect for shallow water and streamy situations. School bass are great fun to catch on fly tackle in skinny water because they hurl themselves at the lure

LURES

Fly fishing is a highly sporting way of catching schoolies, here at the mouth of the Cuckmere River, Sussex.

with such savagery. They slash at the fly repeatedly if they do not get it first time, which is fun to see. Sometimes bigger fish come along as the tide gets under way.

Although I have yet to meet the opportunity, there are places where big bass become preoccupied with very small items of food. Such a place opens bass fishing up to the entire spectrum of the fly fisherman's art. You can tie up attractive representations, and present them with finesse.

The rod can be 8½–10ft long, though I find shorter fly rods better for driving lures into the breeze. You need to be able to do some powerful double-haul casting to reach shoals of bass that are striking baitfish on the fringe of your range. The reel is made from carbon fibre composite, 4in (10cm) wide. It is cheap, reliable and shrugs off salt water, which destroys alloy reels, unless they are washed carefully after use.

I use number 9 shooting heads, and find that a sink-tip, a slow-sinking and a fast-sinking line cover most eventualities. Normally, I use the slow sinker because it gets the lure down far enough in fast, shallow water. In deeper water, the fly swings through too quickly, before it has reached the same depth as the fish, so the fast sinker is necessary. In deep water, 12yds (11m) of lead core trolling line makes a very fine shooting line, and can be cast 40yds (37m) with ease – and a following wind. A more powerful rod is needed to handle it.

Shooting heads can be bought already attached to a backing line. The leader is usually 9ft (2.7m) of 10lb line, but if the weather is very windy, shorten it to 6ft (2m). Occasionally run the leader through your fingers and check for wind-knots, or a big fish may break you.

Waders are handy for providing extra range, or shorts and trainers if the water is warm. A stripping basket is often useful to prevent the line from draping around rocks

Most fly-caught bass are undersized and should be put back.

146

LURES

Kitted up for fly fishing.

LURES

and tangling. You can either buy one or make one from a plastic washing-up bowl. When casting from a steep shingle or rock beach, the loop of the back-cast needs to be flat, rather than the more usual vertical loop, to avoid pinging the streamer on the shingle and snapping off the hook point.

I prefer size 6 hooks with a normal length of shank to stop the long 'wing' from tangling around the hook. I dress the hooks with white goat hair wings and a hot orange throat hackle to suggest damage and blood. The maximum hook size is size 1 because the fly should not be so bulky that it cannot be punched into the breeze. Most fry-type streamers and reservoir lures work well. Lures like the Missionary and Baby Doll all catch bass. For late in the evening, I prefer the Peppermint Doll, with the lime-green fluorescent stripe down its back. Perhaps the bass think it is a tiny squid?

Various designs of flies can be used for bass, but it is better if they are closer to 3in (7.6cm) long than 2in (5cm). It is easy enough to tie up tube flies using squirrel tail, but a white goatskin rug will keep you and your friends in goat hair for years. Alternatively, Delta sandeels and Redgill Rascals can also be fished on fly tackle. At night, black flies or Rascals are useful when the bass are hunting silhouettes.

In deep water, I sometimes use an enormous size 4/0–6/0 'fly' tied from Mylar tinsel. It is rigged and fished in the same way as a large Redgill. Tackle dealers who stock tackle for salmon fishing are a good source of fly-tying materials, and also strong trebles and split rings. They are expensive, but worthwhile. I buy all my fly-dressing materials by mail order from Tom Saville in Nottingham.

DEADBAITS

In the absence of a fly, you might care to try a traditional soleskin lure. It works well wherever bass hunt baitfish. Soleskin lures gleam a translucent blue colour when wet, just like a small fish. First obtain the white skin of a sole from a fishmonger, then stretch it and nail it out on a board. Let it dry before cutting it into willow-leaf shapes. Hook a slip of skin though one end with a carp hook, and fish it on a float, a paternoster (sink-and-draw), or a fly rod.

Some anglers go spinning with dead sandeels, or wobbling with small mackerel. The trouble is that deadbaits give you something else to worry about in hot weather, and it is much more fun to catch fish on artificial lures, particularly if you have made them yourself.

Any fly that looks like a small fish will catch bass.

9 Conservation and the Future for Bass

Bass are such handsome, sporting fish that some anglers prefer to put back every one they catch rather than knock one on the head. Other anglers take a few for the table, and slip the rest back to grow wiser and larger. Commercial anglers kill all fish that are above the 14in (36cm) minimum size (from tip of nose to tip of tail).

Few people were interested in catching bass until the 1970s. Now a bass is a prize that many anglers hope to catch. Since ancient times its firm white flesh has been relished throughout the Mediterranean, but only since the 1980s has it been sought after as a gourmet fish in Great Britain.

The bass's great strength in the underwater jungle is its immense speed at attacking and killing living prey with a single bite to the gills. When bass are convinced that they are onto a good thing, they hurl themselves at baited hooks, and many get caught. Then their strength becomes their weakness. This is sad because they are such strong fish. It is not unusual to catch fish with scars – where they have been gashed by hooks, nets, or sharks – which have healed completely and smoothed over with new scales.

Throughout Britain, there is substantial evidence that once shoals of bass have been hit hard, they do not reappear. Charter skippers from Bradwell caught masses of bass during the 1970s and early 1980s, but in the end there were so few fish that the anglers were complaining. The same has happened on my local patch. Large shoals of bass used to provide us with superlative sport for many years off Beachy Head. In June and July, the birds worked on nearly every tide. The fish could be relied on more often than not, but in 1994, very few were caught.

Such depredations are not reserved solely for the adult fish. In many places, baby bass have been deprived of their nursery areas through the drainage of marshes and the building of marinas, and all the surface oil that they produce. The draining of wetlands, building of barrages, marinas and ports, pollution and so forth have a strong bearing on the ecology of bass nursery areas, and therefore on the survival of the fry during the most critical period of their life cycle. Pollution and alterations to tidal currents affect both the bass and the tiny items of food on which they prey. Fortunately, people have become more aware of the damage that mankind is doing to this planet, so we can count as allies naturalists, environmentalists, birdwatchers and the like.

Thankfully, baby bass are now receiving some measure of protection through the setting up of several nursery areas. No fishing or netting is allowed in these places, and it is hoped this will assist the survival of future generations of bass. The wild card at the moment is global warming. Warmer seas mean faster growth. Baby bass that over-winter in the warm-water discharge from power

CONSERVATION AND THE FUTURE FOR BASS

stations continue growing during the winter, and may end up double the size of fish from the previous year class that have not benefitted from such a favourable environment. If sea levels rise, many wetlands will flood, which should provide the bass with additional nursery areas, but this assumes that a sufficient number of adults will survive to repopulate the sea.

Some large pair trawlers have caught up to forty tons of bass per trip from the torpid shoals that over-winter between Land's End and the Cherbourg Peninsula. This undoubtedly affects the overall stock level and has contributed to the diminishing results of sport fishermen. Bass are facing an onslaught the like of which they have never experienced in millions of years. What is this doing to their social structure? How do the shoals learn the migration routes? We glibly ignore all these questions, yet we know little about where bass go to, and much less about their social structure – and these are long-lived fish.

After years of wandering the ocean, turtles, salmon and a variety of other species, particularly birds, return to lay eggs in the place where they were hatched. Unlike us, they do not require a constellation of GPS satellites to guide them around the ocean. It appears that bass have a similar ability while following their migration routes. Bass fry form into shoals during their first months of life, and the evidence suggests that these shoals stay together for several years and frequent the same areas season after season. Some bass that were tagged on the same day and in the same area

Trawlers can catch more bass in one scoop than I could in a lifetime of angling, but my efforts as a sportsman will have put much more money into the economy.

CONSERVATION AND THE FUTURE FOR BASS

have been caught again together, months later, sometimes during the same fishing session. A 7lb bass that I tagged was caught from the same rock two months later.

Bass that have escaped with a hook in them have been caught days, weeks and months later from the same mark. The hook is recognizable by the pattern, trace, knot, elastic thread or method of sharpening. Often these fish are recaptured by the same angler. It is quite possible that some big bass are only loners because the rest of their shoal has been captured. When commercial anglers hit a mark again and again, nothing is then caught from it for several seasons. Some wrecks are now devoid of bass.

Wrecks are the final stronghold of bass, as they were of cod, but the cod have largely disappeared, and the bass are going the same way. Once anglers start ransacking a fish's final stronghold, catches dwindle alarmingly. Although the secret of hunting is to be so familiar with your quarry's behaviour that you can catch it unawares whenever it suits you, the sporting way to proceed is to be sparing.

THE DECLINE

Few anglers realize that the beaches where they walk, fish, or launch their boats were once remote, undeveloped, and totally undisturbed by people. As recently as fifty years ago, they were home to colonies of terns and nesting gulls. I did not realize it at the time, but I was fortunate to live through the heyday

Putting a bass back. Destined for protection?

CONSERVATION AND THE FUTURE FOR BASS

I was lucky to receive expert tuition from some very talented bass anglers: (left to right) Jim Gibbinson, Ian Gillespie, Dennis Darkin, Clive Gammon and Brian Harris.

of shore fishing. During my lifetime I have witnessed the passing of the birds, and the disappearance of large stocks of fish. Years ago, 100lb-plus common skate could be caught around the Royal Sovereign reef off Eastbourne. Each winter we relied on huge shoals of cod turning up at Dungeness, but these, too, have gone. One night I saw about two tons of cod caught from the beach. I remember feeling miffed because work kept me late, and I only caught 80lb. Most of the other anglers caught double that.

In those days, herring were abundant, and each summer there were swarms of shoaling mackerel close to shore. Anglers on Newhaven Pier frequently hooked thresher shark pups while feathering for mackerel. The beach fishing was very good, and I used to catch lots of black and red bream around an old wooden jetty. Both it, and the bream, have gone. Grandaddy pouting are now rare from inshore reefs. We used to catch lots of them years ago. If they were left out there, congers came along and bit chunks out of them. The remarkable thing is that big bass can still be caught by those who know where to find them.

Shortly after I started bass fishing in 1962, I heard anglers lamenting the fact that they could no longer go and catch a couple of dozen 6–9 pounders from Newhaven East Pier, fishing bunters on the ebbing tide. We didn't realize that it was probably pollution that drove the fish away, because the harbour has always been a busy one, particularly during the War Years.

CONSERVATION AND THE FUTURE FOR BASS

In the late 1960s and early 1970s, my friends and I hardly had blanks and an average evening session usually produced one or two 6–8lb bass, and other bites missed. We also caught good bags of cod consistently from late September through to April. When I first started bassing, I did not need to travel hundreds of sea miles, nor satellite navigation to go and catch a ten-pounder. Now I have to redouble my efforts each season to continue making reasonable catches.

Years ago we used to think that bass lived close to shore and in estuaries, but then anglers discovered vast shoals of them offshore – the Thames Estuary, Beachy Head, the Portland Race, Eddystone and so on. The shoals were so dense and uneducated that they piled into any kind of pirk or feather that looked remotely like food. Huge catches were made, which fuelled the ever-increasing demand for bass by restaurants.

THE COMMERCIAL FISHERY

Pair trawls take the largest catches, sometimes measuring dozens of tons, from the over-wintering stock. Since 1970, commercial catches have doubled, redoubled and doubled again, and that spells trouble for the bass. Pair trawlers, with modern navigational aids, can pin-point precisely where the bass gather. Bass are probably as punctual around their pre-spawning areas as they are while feeding inshore. The threat to the stock is serious and requires prompt attention. It is time a close season was implemented and enforced.

One reason why commercial attention turned to bass was that over-exploitation of traditional species like cod, together with catch quotas, compelled some boats to switch to bass fishing. This was encouraged by the financial rewards. The price climbed inexorably higher until it reached £5.50 per lb.

Twenty to thirty years ago, my friends and I expected to catch fish of this calibre frequently. It's not like that now.

CONSERVATION AND THE FUTURE FOR BASS

Some anglers show scant respect for bass – alive or dead.

As King George VI said: 'The wildlife of today is not ours to dispose of as we please. We have it in trust. We must account for it to those who come after'. Unfortunately, commercial fishermen believe that the wildlife of the sea is their personal property, and they want to exploit it to the point of extinction. Dwindling fish stocks demonstrate the foolishness of this notion.

Many environmentalists question the idea that the seas and their wildlife exist for fishermen to plunder at will. The trouble is that fisheries agreements need to be international since fish recognize no national boundaries. Fishing is a declining industry. The total world catch is dwindling, and even though fishermen are leaving the industry, statistics suggest that the European fleet could be reduced by a third and still produce the same size of catch. With state subsidies being phased out, and tougher laws, fishermen will have to think hard about the economics of ransacking the seas even further.

Unfortunately, some commercial anglers go out of their way to catch large numbers of barely sizeable bass, and overfishing the youngsters before they mature is a foolish way of depleting future stocks. One bass angler told me that because he fished commercially he *had* to snatch small fish. He justifies his infanticide by saying that he has to make a living and pay his mortgage and mooring fees. No doubt this spurious notion allows him to live with his conscience.

Commercial bass fishermen happily feather up hundreds of immature bass that are just

154

CONSERVATION AND THE FUTURE FOR BASS

over the size limit. Not all undersized fish are returned because catches are so rarely inspected. Bagfuls of baby bass are delivered to the backdoors of unscrupulous restaurants. Unless bass are put back alive, they can only be caught once. That does not deter many commercial fishermen from being grotesque optimists. They believe that they can slaughter large numbers of baby bass then catch them again at 8–9lb. Perhaps they believe in reincarnation, but in my experience, once a fish is dead, it stays dead.

FARMING

Thankfully the marketplace looks like coming to the bass's rescue. The thousands of tons of wild bass that have fed the European market in recent years have established a taste for this fine-flavoured fish that is now being catered for by fish farmers. Already the price of farmed bass is pegged below that of wild fish, and as farm production becomes more widespread, the prices that people can charge for wild bass will fall to a level where it is uneconomical for commercial anglers to waste time and fuel chasing such an elusive fish. However, commercial anglers are staying out longer when hitting a shoal of schoolies to catch a greater volume of bass to compensate for the lower price. Even so, it is to be hoped that farmed bass will ultimately help to rescue the wild stock from excessive exploitation.

Bass farming has boomed over the last twenty years. In warm water, and with plenty of food, bass reach ½lb in under a year. The ancient Romans used to collect fry and bring them on in ponds. Now farms in Spain, France, and around the Mediterranean plan to produce hundreds of tonnes each year, with twenty-four hour delivery guaranteed throughout Europe and America. They will be competing on price with fish from Egypt and Tunisia. Salmon farms have already set a precedent for this: in Europe, fifty times more salmon are produced by farms than are caught by rod or net. As a result, salmon is currently cheaper than bass.

For the sport fisherman, this situation is highly desirable. The sooner farmed bass become cheap and widely available the better it will be for the wild stock, making it less cost-effective to pursue them. In 1994 the price of wild bass tumbled.

A young angler looking mighty pleased with his first bass. Farming may save the wild stock for other young anglers.

CONSERVATION AND THE FUTURE FOR BASS

CONCLUSIONS

When pair trawlers net ten tons of bass, some 5,000 large fish cease to be available inshore to provide recreational facilities and alleviate the stress of businessmen and other souls who are the lifeblood of the national economy. Such men are much more likely to put together a tremendous deal after catching a fourteen-pounder than if the sea is devoid of fish.

No government has yet proved capable of justifying the commercial exploitation of sport fish. Very few commercial anglers have made any money out of bass. The cash they receive just about pays their expenses. Despite all the claims to the contrary, most bass fishermen just about manage to break even. In my neck of the woods, two trawlers that made £64,000 out of one hit barely managed to service their bank loans. The following year, one of them was up for sale.

It would be a great treat if politicians would make the effort to do something about the fishing industry. The trouble is that many of their voters are commercial fishermen, and because no party has an overwhelming mandate to take them on, the issue is shelved and the politicians continue to preen in front of the cameras and mirrors, preferring trivia to long-term issues. I spent nine years in Whitehall, and have since met the breed frequently. They do not realize that many more people are involved with catching bass for sport than are in it for commercial gain. They should look to these, the greenest of green voters. I cynically suggest that only a collapse in the stock is likely to draw forth meaningful comments from politicians, which is the only time their comments are ever looked at under a magnifying glass.

Somebody should tell them that any kid who fishes for bass is definitely not mugging old ladies or burgling their homes while he is down on the beach. Oh, for the days when the old timers in Parliament biased fishery legislation in favour of salmon. It is a pity that they overlooked bass. Commercial bass fishing is a transient experience. Each fish exists solely as an instantly forgettable part of the cash flow. The memories for sport fishermen are cherished for a lifetime.

The Irish surf is not as productive as it used to be because the bass stocks were ransacked in the 1970s, with trammel nets everywhere

Ron Preddy caught this ten-pounder, which his young daughter is holding. Will future generations of bass be allowed to survive to such a mature age or will they be exterminated in her lifetime?

CONSERVATION AND THE FUTURE FOR BASS

and trawlers working the surf line. Old gill nets can be seen around Brandon Bay holding down the hay ricks against the wind. A large tonnage of bass was pulled out and sold. Commercial bass fishing in Eire was banned by the Department of the Marine in 1990, and even sport fishing is restricted. Anglers may not keep more than two bass per day and all bass under 16in (40cm) have to be put back alive. There is also a closed season from 15 March to 15 June. These protection measures are a belated acceptance of what everybody has been telling the government for twenty years – live bass in the surf for visiting anglers generate considerably more cash for the local economy than boxes of dead fish. Even so, doubts have been expressed about whether the measures are being observed in a country with such a long history of anarchy.

It is hoped that we have now turned the corner in bass conservation. People are realizing that the resources of the sea belong to everybody. It is no longer acceptable, nor economically justifiable, for a few people to grab the lot. About 250,000 anglers fish for bass around Britain, although only one in ten fishes exclusively for them. Many anglers question whether wild bass should be considered a source of food or whether it should be preserved for recreation. They believe that the economic activity generated by the sport fishery (bait, tackle, equipment, travel, accommodation, mooring fees, boat hire, etc.) is worth considerably more than the input from the commercial fishery.

The conservation movement originally started in the 1970s when Clive Gammon, Brian Harris, Des Brennon, Kevin Linnane

The monofilament gill net has destroyed shore fishing for bass in many areas.

CONSERVATION AND THE FUTURE FOR BASS

and others voiced alarm about declining stocks. This led to the formation of The Bass Anglers Sportfishing Society on 24 March, 1973, and I was there. I recommend all sport fishermen to join BASS and enjoy reading its lively magazine.

People may ask why I have written such a comprehensive book about how to catch bass when the species is under threat. There are two answers to that. The first is that I have spent a huge amount of my life in close contact with bass – either catching them or pondering how to catch them. It would be a waste if all this experience were to go unrecorded. The second answer is that I hope the conservation measures, many of which have yet to be formulated, will ultimately conserve the stock and make bass more widely available as a recreational resource. Perhaps this is the triumph of hope over experience, but I dimly perceive a time when conservation goes hand-in-hand with wise use. There will always be anglers, and I would like to think that others will be able to benefit from my experience, avoid a few of the pitfalls, and hopefully latch into a few lunkers. Only time will tell whether such optimism is justified.

I have been very fortunate that a large number of bass have chosen to take my bait over the years, but the day when I don't get the shakes and a thumping heart after catching a big bass will be the day I stop fishing for them. I hope you have found this book interesting and stimulating. Although I have revealed many secrets, one or two have been left for you to discover. You can't blame me : I want that twenty-five-pounder to take my bait – not yours. Good fishing!

There is a twenty-five pounder down there – somewhere.

158

Index

Aberdeen hooks 48
algal blooms 14, 122
Ambassadeur 46, 116, 122–3
anchor 116–7, 129
antifouling 118
aquaria 89–90, 92, 102
autumn 22, 68

backbone 96
baitclips 34, 129
baitfish 12, 13, 18, 19, 20, 21, 22, 30, 50, 58, 63, 67–8, 70, 78, 93–5, 119, 120, 127, 133, 135, 138, 140–3, 146
baits 12, 18, 55–9, 60–2, 73–4, 77, 79–104
barometer 122
Bass Anglers Sportfishing Society 61, 158
bass
  colour 9
  distribution 9, 17
  dorsal fin 9, 71
  eggs 23
  eyesight 10
  feeding 10, 12, 18–23, 31, 50, 52, 63, 70, 82, 127–8, 136, 140, 149
  fighting 20, 21, 40, 41, 44, 47, 73, 76, 120, 128, 131, 133
  fishing season 17
  fry 20, 23–4, 149, 150
  gills 9, 44
  growth 17, 22–26, 80, 155
  juveniles 14, 17, 21, 24, 155
  lateral line 12, 141
  migration 14–17
  mouth 10, 44
  opercula 9, 26
  over-wintering 10, 17, 25, 150, 153
  predators 12, 24, 149
  sense of hearing 12
  sense of smell 11, 12, 80
  sense of taste 11, 18

sexing 25
shoaling 22
spawning 22–5, 79–80
teeth 128
beach launching 107
beaches 52, 53, 151
  steep 53, 58, 139, 148
bilge pump 117–8
binoculars 112, 114
Biscay bass 14
bite alarms 58
  detection 37–9, 45, 47
bites 19, 20, 29, 35–40, 45, 47, 49, 50, 55–6, 58, 75–6, 79, 81, 129, 133
boats 13, 105–119
boat fishing 30, 76, 119–132, 144
bridges 63–4
bunters 92, 152

Caldy Island 58
calm seas 14, 55, 57–8, 73, 76
camping 61
cast net 98
casting 34, 39, 55, 74–5, 81, 138
charts 68, 111
cheese paste 18, 60
clams 101, 103–4
clear water 31, 40, 52, 57, 96, 99, 102, 127, 133–4
cliffs 78, 135
clothing 50, 54, 116, 124, 134
cloudy water 70, 94, 133–4
coalfish 64
compass 65, 112, 116
commercial angling 151, 153–5
Conoflex 45, 122
conservation 17, 149–58
cool bag 73, 90
crab crusher 85
crabs
  edible 70, 83, 86–8
  general 12, 20, 21, 38, 56, 62, 74, 77, 81, 82–4, 89–91
  hermit 89

shore 84–6
spider 89
velvet swimming 31, 88–9
Cranfield, Nick 31
currents 29, 55, 64, 68, 124, 134, 140
cuttlefish 68, 99, 100

dan buoys 117
deadbait 59, 70, 94–6, 131, 148
Decca navigators 111
deep water 18
diary 50, 111, 135
double-figure bass 25, 26, 63, 86, 119, 127, 129–30
down-rigger 131, 142
drifting 124–9, 131, 135
drop nets 42, 62
Dungeness 61, 104, 116, 152
Dyneema superbraid 47, 136

eels 37, 38, 41, 96, 135
effluent 62, 149
elastic thread 80, 90–1, 104, 123, 151
electronics 109–11
estuaries 13, 14, 18, 45, 52, 62–5, 141

farming bass 155–6
feathers 93–6, 99, 145–8, 153
feeding areas 57, 64, 70, 129
fish finder 67, 95, 109–11, 125–8, 144
float fishing 48, 59, 60, 62–3, 76–7, 92, 102, 131–2, 148
flounders 37
fly fishing 63, 128, 145–8
flying collar 142, 144
forceps 44, 142
free lining 59–60
fresh water 52
fuel 107–9

gaffs 42

159

INDEX

Gammon, Clive 7, 58, 152, 157
Gillespie, Ian 61, 74, 152
Global Positioning System (GPS) 111–2, 150
global warming 10, 24, 149
groundbait 52, 58, 64, 76, 85, 91
gulls and gannets 18, 19, 48, 60, 94, 120–1, 125–7, 134–6, 143, 151

habitats 14
hair rigs 48, 91, 96
harbours 13, 18, 52, 62, 64–5, 78, 111, 141–3
Harris, Brian 58, 61, 74, 152, 157
herring 93, 138, 152
hook sharpeners 48
hooks 10, 39, 40, 44, 46–9, 66, 77, 91–2, 99, 100, 123, 136, 138, 141-2, 144, 148, 151

ice 90
International Perfection 709 118

jerry cans 107–8

Kelley, Donovan 8
knots 44, 47, 94, 96, 123, 129, 138

Ladle, Dr Mike 140
landing bass 11, 42, 44, 55, 71, 141
  net 42, 44, 124, 142
landmarks 109, 112
lead clips 49
  weights 49, 73, 95, 123, 131, 138, 143
leaders 47, 48, 73
ledges 57, 58, 64
lifejackets 65, 78
lights 11, 49
line 11, 38, 39, 44, 46–48, 124, 134, 136–8, 143
livebaits 19, 20, 60, 62, 77, 81, 93, 95, 100, 126–9, 131
livebait tank 95, 117
lobster pots 18, 68
logbook 111–2
lugworm 21, 74, 100, 102–2
Lureflash 94
lures 62, 78, 124, 125, 128, 131, 133–148

mackerel 12, 19, 21, 32, 53, 55, 58, 62, 64, 77, 93–7, 125, 128, 135, 143, 148, 152
maggots 104
match fishing 33, 81
Mesmer, Eric 36, 91, 96
Moncrieff, Les 61
Mustad 48, 91, 100, 104

navigation 109–12, 153
nursery areas 23, 24, 98, 149

octopus 100
offshore fishing 13, 18, 21
O'Kennedy, Dennis 20
outboard engines 106, 117, 131
out-riggers 131–2

pheromone 84
piers and jetties 13, 33, 34, 44, 57, 60–6, 92, 98, 139, 142, 152
pirks 95, 125, 137, 140, 142, 144–5, 153
plug fishing 13, 20, 31, 34, 63, 70, 76, 131, 138, 140-3
pollack 21, 64–5, 125, 128, 135, 138, 142
pollution 149
poor cod 98, 138, 142
pouting 27, 38, 59, 61–2, 64, 74, 98, 138, 141–2, 152
prawns 40, 62–4, 76–7, 92, 136
priest 50, 124
psychological moment 31, 38

radar 109
ragworms 22, 62, 77, 102
razorfish 20, 101, 103–4
Redgills 64, 120, 131, 138, 142–4, 148
reefs 13, 31, 53, 67–78, 98, 120, 124, 139, 140, 143
reels 44, 45, 46, 59, 134, 136
reel drag 35, 131, 136
  maintenance 47, 117, 123
RNLI 105
rock ledges 30, 31, 67–78, 86–8, 122, 126, 131–3
rods 36, 40, 44–46, 48, 61, 63, 73, 78, 136
rod rests 35, 46, 73, 95, 131
ropes 116
rough seas 34, 68, 92, 116

safety 65–6, 78, 88, 114–6, 142
sand 55, 57
sandbanks (and shingle) 64
sandeels 60–4, 77, 98–9, 128, 135, 148
sand hoppers 104
scad 64
scale reading 26
school bass 34, 37, 50, 62, 96, 125, 128, 135, 145, 155
seamanship 115
seine netting 15, 99
shallows 57–8, 135
shrimps 21, 92

Sikaflex 221–2
slaters 104
slipper limpet 104
smoked salmon 104
snags 41, 47, 75–7, 134, 140, 144
soleskin lures 148
south-east coast 25, 40, 68, 71, 105, 134, 149
spinners 13, 63, 138–40
spinning 19, 20, 31, 34, 50, 62, 70, 76, 139
sprats 18, 55, 61, 64, 139
spying 112, 132
squid 12, 53, 62, 68, 77, 99, 100, 148
striking 35, 37, 39, 40, 56, 76
structure 52, 57, 63–4, 76, 111, 124, 128–9
sunglasses 50, 115, 138
surf 13, 28, 33, 35, 39, 41, 49, 51, 52, 53–5, 64, 68, 70, 121–2, 136
swivels 49, 61

tackle 44–9, 55, 60, 63–4, 71–3, 122–4, 129, 136–8, 143–6
tagging 15, 150
temperature 14, 23, 24, 80, 86
Thames estuary 15, 149
tide chart 50, 65–6, 71
tides 14, 15, 19, 26, 29, 31, 33, 39, 49, 53, 57, 62–4, 70, 74, 92
tools 115
traces 38, 39, 48, 49, 77, 91, 143
trawlers 15, 80, 105–6, 141, 150–3, 156–7
trolling 95, 131–2, 139, 143

unhooking 44
up-tide casting 13, 129–131
Upol-B 109

VHF radio 114
vingler 98

waders 50, 53, 134, 146
warm water 61
weather conditions 29, 31, 114
weed 55, 60, 64, 141
weighing 49, 50
whelks 104
wooden blocks 108–9
wrasse 37, 73, 135, 138, 142
wrecks 52, 68, 106, 111, 119, 121–4, 126–8, 151

year classes 24, 25

Zziplex 45

160